WOMAN

WHAT HAVE YOU DONE

MIKA RACE

For inquiry or wholesale, please contact Mika at mikarace@icloud.com

ISBN: 979-8-9872564-8-0 Paperback
ISBN: 979-8-9894166-0-8 Hardback
ISBN: 979-8-9872564-9-7 Ebook

Dedication

First, I would like to say thank you to my two children,
Douglas and Kristie. Without their constant support and love,
I would not have written this book. They are my biggest die-hard
fans and believe in me like none other. Being their mother is my
greatest accomplishment in life.

To my husband, Doug, my story's knight in shining armor.
We were two kids without any idea what our future held, but
God knew. He saw our end from the beginning, and I'm forever
grateful to be your wife. Without you, the story falls apart.
P.S. As I always tell you, you keep holding my feet down,
but I'll always keep you flying.

To my grandchildren, my legacy. Lexy, Justus, Jackson,
Bentley, and Ocean. You are the jewels in my crown.

Acknowledgments

I want to thank Blake Bennett, who introduced me to Courts of Heaven by Robert Henderson. She unveiled a whole new world for me, and finally, I had language for what I knew already; I'm eternally grateful to her and her podcast, The Dreamseers.

To Steve and Ginny Maddox, who said yes to the email of someone they did not know to pray and impart to me on my 50th birthday, especially to Ginny, who has taken me under her wing so lovingly as a spiritual mother. Divine connections are just that–divine. God orchestrates your destiny before you are born and puts those people in your life who are connected to your destiny to get you to your destiny.

INTRODUCTION 1

UNDISTURBED 5

INVISIBLE SHAPERS 19

NEEDING HOPE 31

REDEEMER 45

WHEN GOD CALLS US 57

PURGE THE DARK SHADOWS 69

COMING OUT OF THE CAVE 83

LIFE OF REDEMPTION 95

WOMEN FULL OF WONDER 109

Introduction

We're not too different, you and I. We've all been through the great and terrible. When you look at my wounds, you can see what made me or at least that is my hope. For years, I would only identify with the pain in my past. My best friend was the afflictions I laid upon myself and those that were laid upon me. I had no guide to show me how I should live and think correctly. I didn't realize what I was made of or whom I belonged to. So, I did not know any other reality other than misery and bondage with a lack of identity and poor self-worth. I learned to walk very well with my limp.

I couldn't find words to describe my emotional state early in my life. Perhaps I was numb. The situation that surrounds my life brought me to difficult and unthinkable circumstances. I felt left alone with no guide except the shame and guilt in my life to nudge me along. I was sitting on a plane by myself at fourteen flying to meet my soon-to-be husband, Doug, flying away from my family and everything I had known. I don't remember much about that day other than the fact that I would take any reality over the dysfunction I was living in.

Forty years passed, and I realized that I was not too different from the other women in the world. Shame kept me from hiding from my true calling. The emotional pain of my past and my mind prevented me from doing anything significant with my heart. I was stuck behind the lies, shame, and the doubts that I told myself and that others told me. My life was not my own; I felt powerless more than I felt powerful. This sentiment is far too common among women; therefore, this affliction has an equal adversary in our divine potential.

My entire world turned upside-down when I realized I could live differently. I understood the unique challenges women face daily because I lived, thought, and felt them. The heavy yolks that I accepted as my own restricted me from becoming the person I was born to be. I'm not just talking about doing great things in life. I'm talking about being free. I pursued becoming true to myself, so that lies could no longer hold me in chains and bondage.

After revisiting the monuments, the mountains, and the obstacles in my life, I look out and see that my story is not just my own. My story was for everyone because, in my trials, many can relate, and we're not too different. Before I could get prideful thinking that I was so special going through something so unique, I realized there's a greater source from which all of this comes. Her name is Eve, the mother of all. She embodies the journey of a woman. Her name and its definition are the source of life. She sets the standard for the common woman.

Everyone's familiar with her story in some way or another, but very few understand the situations that surround the source of her life. The commonalities and correlation within the life of Eve that echo into every area of our humanity are unparalleled. Eve embodied what it meant to be human. She became a divine symbol and a marker for our relationship with God. Her trials and perplexities were far too familiar to overlook. When we look at Eve, we see ourselves. She is, in fact, where we get our traits from.

Our lives and the journey of Eve have far too much in common. I humbly say that because I think we are straightforward people deep down inside. Those things that bind her and inhibit her true expression have gone unchanged since the beginning of time. We wake up every day trying to find our sense of purpose and our identity. Of course, we all struggle with the situations and circumstances that life gives us. We choose paths that place us in harm's way. Sometimes we don't choose a path at all because we don't want to make any more bad choices.

Every woman embodies the capabilities to create through her sensitive, subtle, powerful, and outspoken demeanor. Because we embody our thoughts and feelings so much, we feel the severity of humanity in its emotional state and its delicate balance much more than men typically do. This is why we need to approach a woman's journey and its ups and downs in a way that brings us wholeness, so that we may find ourselves and live out our true purpose today.

Join me in this pursuit to find your identity in all the chaos. If you're searching for significance amid indecision, if you feel trapped in life and want to hide from becoming something for someone—perhaps you've been labeled or self-identified with something far less than your worth—then this journey is for you. Let us go on a path together. To overcome, to redeem, to find Healing.

You are invited into unbridled creativity, freedom, and redemption. We have the potential to produce life in everything that we do. It's what we were born for. Our sensitivity and grace shouldn't be stolen with doubts and lies. We are worth far more than we can imagine, and once we find our place or identity, then we will live unbound and redeemed. Thank you for embarking on this journey with me in the pursuit of significance, truth, and meaning. I truly hope that you're able to see yourself in my story.

Undisturbed

E very good story starts in the beginning. Where did life begin? Was it some uncontrolled explosion, or was it a miraculous creation? The very concept of life's origin seems simple and unrelated, but it's not. It testifies to our present confusion. We don't fully know who we are, and therefore, we don't know whom we belong to. When we search our hearts, we are sometimes unsettled about our life's meaning, purpose, and identity. This is nothing new under the sun. These are the same self-interpretations and reflections that have come up with every woman since the beginning of time. Are we led by our feelings or our intellect? What parts of us are special and unique? Perhaps it's hard to see all that now because we sometimes feel like wandering stars on a cloudy night. Never mind the comprehension of our lives now with their complexities and nuances, the perception of our past and failures mixed with our double-mindedness and fears.

What if we were to start at the beginning? What if we consider life before every label, opinion, and obstacle? That would bring us to the beginning. Every one of our journeys starts off the same. We all had an explosive entry into a world that we never knew before we crossed into the veil of this life on earth. The thoughts of our parents and some majestic blueprint fashioned us. This blueprint worked in our mothers to build out the inner parts of ourselves. It spoke to our cells and told them which way they should grow so our arms would go in the right direction and our heads would end up in the right place. We were beautifully and wonderfully made.

While in the womb, we were untouched, unadulterated, naked, and pure. We were unaffected by the outside world. In the beginning, the only thing we knew was to exist in our immaculate design and nothing else. Bask with me in this. You have no name by which people call you. No opinion has been fashioned against you. You are free to be and free to become. You have no social constraints, no financial burdens, and no limitations. You embody hope and promise that you will soon encounter a brand-new world. This is how everyone starts their journey, pure and unaffected by anyone or anything. It's easy to get lost in the consideration of being unbound by everything. The thought of this unborn baby resting in peace, in need of nothing. It makes me get lost in the vastness of unending awe.

We See as We Are Not as We Should

The pure and unadulterated world that we were once in quickly became a distant dream after we crossed that veil into life. We are born into a family that issues freedoms and restrictions based on how they see fit. We are given a name based on who they want us to be. We are brought up the way that they see the world. Some are born into tremendous promise, while others are brought forth into difficulty and struggle. We don't see the world as it should be; we see the world as we are. The way that we process our lives and our past determines our perceptions about those around us and our environment. We embody the situations that surround us when we are vulnerable and pliable as children. Every situation has the potential to mark us for life because we are so malleable and undecided in how we should perceive the world and the people around us.

Some of my earliest memories dictated my thoughts and ideals for most of my life. It set me on a course to behave in particular ways and become reactionary to the world around me. One of my first memories I can recall is when I was six. I was standing on the porch with my siblings and my mother. We were crying, begging my father not to leave us. As the orange van pulled up to take my father to the airport that night, I had no way of knowing I would bury that memory for decades. It's as though I had put that memory in a box and left it in a pitch-black room. When I attempted to comprehend the severity that night played in forming me at six and how it affected my whole life, my world was crushed like a pile of bricks falling from the sky. It was almost as if every past memory was wiped away because this one was so wounding.

For that moment, my world had ended because the harmony I once knew, as convoluted as it was, was gone. My image of family and my father was wrapped in chaos. When you're young and you lose stability from those who support you, words can't describe how to comprehend those life moments. They impact your soul and mark you for every future year. The emotional trauma was so great that I bottled it up inside like still water begging for oxygen.

My father was a gypsy man who was always running from the demons of his past. He was enlisted in the Army at eighteen and went to Vietnam that year. When he came home from Vietnam, he was a different man than the one his family knew. Alcohol became his vice. Short-term and short-sighted was how he approached life and relationships. My siblings and I became experts in packing quickly. We were always on the move, moving just about every six months. We never ended a school season where we started. The announcement came that we were moving, and that's exactly what happened. We didn't have a choice in the matter. I didn't get time to say goodbye to my friends, let alone did I get time to make new friends, because we left each place so quickly. In each of those homes, we left far more than material belongings; fragments of ourselves remained behind. I guess in a sense I thought it was normal to leave everything except what would fit in your car because it was our normal. I remember so many times coming home and finding all of our furniture turned upside-down. At times, I was awakened from my sleep by my father yelling, "Shoot me, shoot me." He was having flashbacks of Vietnam and would be hiding behind the kitchen table or coffee table he'd turned over. I learned what fear felt like from him. I would lie in my bed scared to death to move, so I didn't. Even at fifty, I still can be lying in my bed and feel that same fear. At times, it takes my breath away, and instantly, I'm that little girl again.

Often, we would move somewhere with no money and no place to go. We would live in a tent or camper in the beginning, while my mother would find a job and save enough for housing. As you can imagine, when you live in a camper or a tent on the beach, you don't have much comfort and sometimes you have no electricity or water. And, yes, we lived on the beach in a tent. With no money, you park where it's free, right? I remember one day when I was maybe ten, we were living in a tent on the beach in Texas, and it was raining very hard. I was trying to sweep the rain out of the tent because our blankets and what little clothes we had were getting wet. I remember the dampness, the smell, and the words I spoke out loud for the first time in my life. I looked up and said, "Please let him die." I repeated it over and over. That was the defining moment in my life. It would've been much easier if my father were dead. At least then he wouldn't keep putting us through the hell in which we lived. The tears came like buckets that day. No ten-year-old should be sweeping rain out of a tent so their belongings don't get wet. One day while in school, a boy tapped me on the shoulder and showed me a piece of paper that had the words "tent girl" written on it with a drawing of a tent. Even at ten, humiliation is an arrow straight to the heart. I have never shared that till now.

It didn't matter what state we moved to; my parents were still going to behave the exact same way, thus resulting in no actual change except the trauma that me and my siblings lived in. Of course, my experience was hard to verbalize at such a young age, but today, I am able to put it into words. The fear of the unknown was abounding. My siblings and I felt a tremendous sense of unsettledness and lack of stability. When one of your parents leaves, part of yourself is gone with them.

You see, after my father left us at six, he eventually came back, only to leave us again and again. My mom was perhaps the most traumatized by it all. Her trauma was materialized by verbal and physical abuse at the hands of my father. He never laid his hands on me, but he would beat my mother in front of us kids. She feared him tremendously. Perhaps she was his punching bag for the pain that he was experiencing. Nevertheless, she was helpless. Maybe she thought staying was for the betterment of her family. Perhaps it was all she had known. See, her dad left her and her siblings when she was three, washed his hands of his family, and called it a day.

I might never know that answer of why she stayed because my mother is like a glass bottle floating at sea with the S.O.S. still inside it, bottled up tighter than a drum. I imagine her pain became so great that her number one coping strategy was to become numb, and when you're numb, you sweep every affair, every blow, every crushing word under the rug as though it never happened. You blame yourself for every time you're abused because, indeed, you did something wrong to deserve it. We learned to walk on eggshells around my father because we did not want to trigger him in any way.

One Friday night, my mother and us kids went to the bar to get his paycheck before he spent it all on alcohol. As we sat in the car waiting for her to return, we saw her running and my father running behind her. She jumped in the car and threw it in reverse, but it was too late; he punched her repeatedly in her face as she tried to get away. I was in the passenger seat crying and screaming, "Stop, stop!" as loud as I could. But it never stopped him before, so this time was no different. My siblings and I witnessed his abuse toward our mother more times than I would like to remember. From choking her against the wall to sitting on top of her beating her face black and blue, we were the witnesses to every attack.

She taught us never to say anything because if you don't talk about the elephant crushing you, it doesn't exist, right? She had lived in survival mode her whole life. What do you do with abuse, affairs, and poverty? There are no good options available. If you stay, you keep the family intact together and become a doormat. If you leave, you're certain to have a broken family. Our family was already broken in a million shattered pieces, but she couldn't see it. I guess she hoped to have the family together. Broken, yes, but at least together. However, this path of least resistance came with extended and prolonged pain. So, what does a six-year-old do but mirror the same coping strategy as their parents? I learned how to bottle every emotion down deep inside so well that it took me almost forty years to unpack them and start to let some light in that dark room.

Numbness would surround me in my mind, heart, and actions. When you don't know what to do, becoming numb is a realistic solution at such a vulnerable age. Once I could comprehend some of my feelings as I got older, I felt a tremendous sense of shame because now I had a broken home and no friends to be a child around. Going out, making friends, and having fun was not on the agenda. My emotional baggage continued to mount as the dysfunction continued.

I would sit and watch my mom and ask myself, why isn't she leaving? Why is she enduring such a painful process? Of course, I couldn't understand or comprehend the situation's complexities, but you just want to run away from the pain. The pain started to grow in me as well. The only natural process for this bottled-up, prolonged emotional pain was to hate my father. I hated him for what he was doing to me and what he was doing to my mom and my siblings. Because of his choices, my childhood was robbed of joy and stability, but mostly peace. The simple peace of lying down and feeling secure. You can only imagine how one would set their world views after experiencing such things.

We're Not Too Different

After spending years unpacking the emotional baggage of my past, I realized we all have a lot in common. We women sort of go through the same things. Perhaps it's because we are uniquely made to be similar, and therefore, we process life together. Perhaps it's because we encounter the same world and the same kinds of people. Most definitely, we go through the same arc and struggles. We have the same emotions and the same thoughts about life. We're all trying to fit in, find ourselves in this big world, and find our sense of meaning and belonging. At the end of the day, we all want to be loved by ourselves and by those around us. Realizing our commonalities, I thought to look first at the origin of life. Perhaps we'll find something there that will shed some light on our overlapping experiences.

There's a lady named Eve. She is said to be the source of life For All Mankind. That's what her name means. She was the first woman to walk the earth according to God; her story is quite interesting. In Genesis 1:26, Mankind is made in the image and likeness of God. It's undisputable the meticulous detail in which we're created. God is said to have placed Mankind inside of Adam, in whom He made male and female. No doubt, it's hard to consider God placing both male and female inside of Adam, but I guess it makes sense when we think of how we get pregnant. It's like Adam. This unified being that God created had the potential to create life within himself. We see that is evident in our own lives today, and therefore, it's easier to comprehend.

A few days pass by, and God is in search of a helper for Adam. He then makes all of the animals and beasts beforehand to ensure that Adam doesn't find a helper in all of them. Adam still needs a helper once all the animals and the insects are created. So, God looks to Adam, places him in a deep sleep, and then Fashions Eve out of one of Adam's ribs. This was the case because God wanted Adam and Eve to be divinely connected. Adam said it best when he looked at Eve and said, "Bone of My Bone and Flesh of My Flesh." They were one. Their unity brought them together in more ways than they could comprehend. They weren't two separate individuals. They were one according to God. So, interestingly, when God looked at Adam and Eve, He saw one person because they were unified in the flesh. They looked at each other for the first time, were both naked, and felt no shame.

If we were to analyze their innocence for a moment, we would quickly conclude that they lived in a blissful state. They walked the earth naked with no shame for a particular amount of time. No opinion was cast over them that told them otherwise. They lived in perfect harmony with no opposing force to take that away. They weren't given any labels or social constraints. They had an abundance of everything they could ever want. They lacked nothing. Even though they were naked, they were content with who they were because nothing challenged their sense of self and their identity. When they looked at each other, they only saw what was good because only good was introduced to them at this point.

The ideas of failure and brokenness were not introduced yet. Therefore, they felt no shame in who they were or what they were about. They were content in their thoughts and their hearts. There was no need for them to hide from anything because they only knew good and each other. Clothing wasn't even considered because they were transparent in each other's eyes. They only saw Beauty and good in themselves and in their partner. Imagine a life of endless possibilities without the introduction of evil. This, too, is how we entered the world from our unborn state.

Now, we've all heard the story a million times. Eve was tricked into eating from the tree that she was commanded not to eat from. She inherently knew this because she came from Adam, even though that commandment was given before she was created. I'm sure Adam promptly shared all of the Commandments with Eve upon her creation and made sure that she was well aware of her one constraint in life: not to eat from the Tree of Good and Evil. Perhaps Adam forgot to share that important detail.

The cunning and crafty serpent came over to Eve and challenged God. Did God really say, "You must not eat from any tree in the garden"? Eve knew the Commandment of God was not to eat from the tree; she even added extra details, like the fact that she wasn't even allowed to touch the tree. The serpent challenged her understanding and said if she were to eat from the tree, she would be like God, knowing Good and Evil. So, she reconsidered the lie even though she was already like God and saw it was pleasing and desirable to her eyes. She probably shared this with her husband, and he ate from the tree as well.

As soon as they consumed the fruit of Good and Evil, their eyes were opened, and their world changed. See, Adam and Eve didn't have any context for evil beforehand. Now, suddenly, they were filled with it. It was now a part of them. Their eyes became open to a world filled with evil that clashed with good. This world quickly overwhelmed them because now they had to manage a life filled with evil. This was God's one request not to partake in this understanding lest it overcome them. It happened anyway. It was destined to happen. They quickly realized they both were naked, so they sewed fig leaves together to cover themselves.

Imagine the flood of evil coming into a good vessel, dividing every thought into good and bad and every emotion into good vs. evil. Imagine the shock and awe their physical bodies endured when evil entered. Their sense of self and stability was overrun by this foreign body, the pervasiveness of evil. It was so overwhelming that it immediately changed their minds about their identities and each other. They quickly left their pure and unadulterated States and were overrun with the reality of evil and the future of death. When they looked at each other, they wanted to hide. That is why they made their clothes for the first time. They felt shame in who they were and what they saw because their sense of self and their identity was shaken.

It's quite ironic the way that God reintroduced Himself into the scene. Adam and Eve heard the sound of God as they were walking in the garden in the cool of the day. This was supposed to be another day of paradise, just like those before it. Instead, the evil within them compelled them to hide from God. They were trying to hide from themselves and their Creator. God called out to them and said, "Where are you?" I imagine they probably didn't know because everything was so different now. Adam responded to God and said, "I heard you in the garden, and I was afraid because I was naked, so I hid."

Disturbed

Everything inside of Adam and Eve at the time repelled what was holy and pure. They only spoke from a reality that they could not yet comprehend or manage. They feared everyone and everything because of the fears that dwelled within them. Perhaps they couldn't even recognize that God had created them, and that therefore, He was fully acquainted with who they were and what they looked like, just as a mother is acquainted with her child. Their realization of their nakedness was a testament to their mental state. Every sense of innocence that they once had was now gone. They felt alone and broken because of their understanding of evil.

This, too, is the world that we were born into. Once we crossed that veil into our first breath, we put on good and evil. The labels of life and social constraints were quickly put upon us. We were named something to behave a particular way for our parents' sake. We became judged instantly for the way that we looked and behaved. Our worlds were quickly filled with the idea of an unsettled reality.

Somehow, we are supposed to find our purpose and meaning amid the complexities and obstacles that entangle us. If only we were lucky to be loved unconditionally initially and have a perfect childhood, we may be set on a successful path, but for many, that is not the case.

We all may have different paths, but our realities remain the same. Our challenges with ourselves and with the world around us all come from the same place. Down inside, we hope to be found. We hope to be loved. We hope to live a life unbound. However, this is not the world that we know. We are overtaken and confused by the things that challenge us. We have forgotten the place of eternal peace that we came from.

Invisible Shapers

When your heart's broken into multiple pieces, you will do anything to prevent more pain from happening. You may attempt to deploy certain coping strategies or convince yourself that your heart is not broken. You may say it just bleeds a little daily, but it is nothing to worry about. This, too, was the case for me. I could naturally assume that the traditional fight, flight, or freeze was in store, but because I was in no shape to fight, I chose the latter two options. I froze inside and decided to fly away. I placed all my emotions on ice to preserve what was left of my heart.

Sure, I still tried to have fun and live life, but there were parts of me that I definitely kept numb. I was constantly looking for a way to end my internal conflicts, so running away seemed like a perfect solution. Subconsciously, I was planning my escape at thirteen years old when I met a guy named Doug through my sister. We lived in Ohio at the time and talked over the phone for six months. My family moved to Texas not long after we met, and I eventually ran away to be with him. I bought and paid for a flight from Texas to Ohio when I was fourteen to be with him. At the time, there were no flight restrictions for fourteen-year-olds. No parental consent or handoff was necessary. As I was waiting there at the gate, ready to board my flight, I knew what I was doing. I was surviving. I was running. Sure, I tried to convince myself that I wasn't running away from my past, but I was. I was desperate for a new world and reality that gave me hope and life.

At fourteen, your mind thinks for the now, not forever, right? I lied to him for a year about how old I was. I was desperate for stability and genuinely fell in love with him early on–well, if, at fourteen, you know what love is. I did everything I could to position myself to be won over. Do you blame me? Any life I was trying to create seemed better than the one I'd left. Of course, my family didn't chase me when I left. It was as though I was not a part of their day-to-day rhythm of life. Or even worse, I was a vapor here today, gone tomorrow. Maybe they did not know how and justified it. That one single act from my parents no doubt shaped my life forever. It still haunts me even as I write about it all these years later.

With no one else to lean on, I sought the support of my beautiful grandmother, Mae. She was one of the few constants in my childhood. She was a woman of little stature, and maybe weighed 100 pounds soaking wet. However, her love for us kids was as high as the heavens. Her first husband left her for another woman when my mother was three. She then married an alcoholic, a very verbally and at times abusive man. She worked in a meat factory. We would visit on her lunch break. I still remember the steam from her piping-hot thermos of Lipton chicken noodle soup. She said it warmed her bones after being in the meat freezer all day.

Seeing her coming up the path to our door with groceries in her hands after my father left us was our lifeline. So, it was no surprise for me to reach out to her after I flew back to Ohio. When I turned fifteen, my boyfriend, Doug, and I started looking for ways to get married because we were ready to begin a new life. It was against the law in Ohio, so we went to Virginia and got married with the acceptance and approval from my grandmother, which was required.

I was on a fast track to build my family because it gave me structure and meaning. I didn't feel it was wrong to do so. Perhaps it was the best thing that I could do given my circumstances. I realize now the things that compelled me to do what I did were directly tied to how I associated myself with my past. My family always ran away from their demons, and here I was, running away. My mother also married young, and here I was, married young. Moving out of the house at such a young age of fourteen is not normal in today's culture and society. Getting married so young is not a normal thing to do. There are reasons why people typically wait until their brain is fully developed before doing something like that.

Martha

I often look to the women of the Bible for context on their lives and associations. It intrigues me to look at how they were portrayed and how they handled certain situations. I have an inkling that tells me there's some type of comprehensive picture here. Perhaps each woman in the Bible tells you a unique story in which they all fit together. Allow me to introduce you to a woman in the New Testament that we're all too familiar with. You may not know her name, but I'm sure you can relate to who she is. Her name is Martha. She's a woman for which maybe faith didn't come very easy. Maybe she'd been through a lot. Maybe she saw the world a certain way because of her past. For whatever reason, her storyline was a great juxtaposition next to Mary and Jesus. She often preferred duty over relationships, work over rest, and striving over contentment. One time, she said to Jesus, "Lord, do you not care that my sister is not helping me?" (Luke 10) Haha! Martha thought that she could get God to help her with her manipulative tactics. We laugh at her, but we've all done it.

We see Martha, and most of us see ourselves. We know our flaws, and they keep us from resting. We strive to always be doing something because we know we don't deserve better; at least, we think we don't. We survive and compel others to help us keep our emotional head above the water. Not because we are being forcibly held down but because we don't know the way up. We need help; we need direction and love.

Ideally, Martha could have behaved the exact same way that Mary did and simply enjoyed Christ's company, but she couldn't. She was distracted by the things that bound her. She was compelled by the invisible things that shaped her. Her mind and heart and her perceptions kept her from enjoying the moment. We all know Martha too well. That's because we are Martha. We're constantly trying to find ways to fix our problems, realizing that we are barely keeping it together.

We tell ourselves that if we can do better next time, then they'll love us. I would have been accepted if I had only said something differently. Perhaps, if I behave a little differently, then I will be received. Maybe if I convince them I'm more whole than I am, then I will become that. All the work, sweat, and emotional toil don't bring us what we hope to achieve. It's all striving for more. It's all surviving. It's the only thing we know to do. We're convinced to behave a certain way regardless of how the world treats us. It doesn't matter what you do. We'll find ways to justify why we believe the way we do. It's because we're broken and flawed inside. Even if we're loved, we don't believe it. There's no place for the love to go because the vessel is broken. Even if we're in the presence of someone who provides unconditional love, we won't receive it.

This was the case for Martha as well. Jesus said that he had unconditional love for her, yet she still strived to feel it. Maybe, for the first time in her life, she was shown that there was more than one option. On one occasion, he called her name out twice, "Martha, Martha." It was as if he was trying to get her to snap out of it. When we're bound by things inside, numb to the outside world, we're more robotic and less emotional in the things we do. This is because we've been hurt too many times. We'd prefer to be about our work and not our love because we no longer want to be judged or let down. It's so much easier to clock in and clock out than truly engage and let someone know the inner parts of ourselves and get to know the deep and meaningful places in our lives. We'd prefer to keep them on the outside. We tell ourselves that they won't hurt us if we don't let them in. You won't have to process the pain anymore because you didn't let them in.

We stand next to these people we say we love, but we're not honest with them because we're not honest with ourselves. We convince ourselves that we're justified in lying. Our situation requires us to continuously tell white lies to ourselves. We say nobody knows what we've been through. Nobody can even relate to the pain and suffering that we've experienced. We are the ultimate victims. We are exalted in victimhood in every justification for staying exactly the way that we are. Yes, great and awful things have been done to us and around us. We have every justification under the sun to behave the way we do. No one's going to take our scars away. We are fighters; we are survivors. We will die with these badges of honor if it is the last thing we do. We are Marthas.

Check Your Pulse

Every once in a while in life, we slow down enough to check our pulse. Deep down inside, we all know we have a heartbeat; we just want to see if we can detect a rhythm. Why do we do this? I think it's because we need to check in with ourselves to realign our bodies with our emotions and our perceptions. It's like when we stop breathing and pay attention to every breath. We open our airways, feel the air go into our lungs, and then we exhale. The process within itself is very calming because we're grounding our body and our mind to something. We do not need to do this every time we breathe because our body and mind do it for us. We don't even need to pay attention to this process at all because it operates in a completely different way subconsciously.

We, too, operate subconsciously within the parameters of our perceptions, values, and past experiences. We often don't know that there are invisible realities that affect who we are daily. These constructs are not just a figment of our imagination; they are belief systems, value systems, traumatic experiences, and personal agreements that puppet us throughout the day. We behave a certain way because we believe a certain way. This is not a justification for cause. We're not looking for anybody to blame, necessarily. We just want to be whole. We want to be rid of our junk and baggage so we can move on with life.

The first step into this next season takes tremendous courage. It requires looking at those invisible realities that shape us from within. What made us who we are today? What situations define our present realities? What kinds of people and their failed or successful coping strategies affect how we see the world? What belief systems define how you perceive the world?

At This Stage in My Life

Now, I can see the invisible things that shaped me in my mind and my heart. They acted as a guide that led me to make certain decisions about how to approach the world and cope with my feelings about myself. I made spoken and unspoken resolutions with myself to justify my feelings. They bound me. In some instances, I was persuaded to run. In other cases, I felt persuaded to go numb and not let any feelings come in or go out. I concluded that if I shut down my ability to produce emotions, then I wouldn't get hurt anymore. Sometimes, I felt fearful of people, the unknown, and my past. Most of all, I wanted to hide because I felt shame about who I was, where I came from, the dysfunction in my family, and some of my decisions.

Of course, at the time, every thought, feeling, and decision was made in self-preservation. They were sugar-coated in justification and cause, which is not always wrong. I did what I had to do to give myself a chance, even though I was running from something instead of running toward something. Any situation can be laced with good, but when we start a process because of an unhealthy reason, we are driven by it. The fuel that keeps the process going might produce good, but it inherently comes from an unhealthy place.

If a person chooses to love another out of fear of abandonment, fear of lack, and fear of significance, is their love pure? They pursue love; is it wholesome and pure? Or is their love diluted or infected because of its motivating source? The intention one has, and even the outcome one might achieve, is not the basis on which we measure ourselves. There's always more than meets the eye, and we should be aware of these invisible realities that shape the world we live in and how we think and feel. They make up who we are more than our accomplishments or accolades. How are we actually doing if we're surviving inside and everything around us is doing just fine?

We can believe a certain way or mistreat ourselves for some great noble cause if we strip away all the fluff and be honest with ourselves. Chipping away at our exterior shell is painful. Over the years, we built up such a protection around who we are and why we think the way we do. We've told each other things that we know are to protect our hearts. We think we've got them convinced that we are a certain way. We've got them fooled into believing things we know aren't true about us. Perhaps we've convinced them that we have it all together. We are satisfied in our own skin and absolutely happy with who we've become. We know the truth. That's why it's hard to look at ourselves in the mirror for too long—because we start to see what we believe about ourselves.

We start to realize the only person that we fooled was ourselves. Our tricks and schemes and half-truths didn't go very far. The only thing we got from them was more emotional pain because now we have to cover it up with some more lies. The only way through is to be true to ourselves. We must be honest with ourselves about our beliefs and our thoughts. Raw, transparent honesty is so hard because we've Justified it for so long. We've come up with a million reasons why we shouldn't confront the truth and move on. Maybe we feel like we've done it for so long that there's no way back, but there is; there's always a way home.

Suppose you were to analyze your thoughts on a daily and weekly basis. How many of those thoughts come from the retelling and rehashing of past situations? How many thoughts speak to your intention today to try and get the most out of your current situation? Lastly, how many of those thoughts are specifically tied to the hope of your future and are geared toward planning it out accordingly?

Are you currently participating in anything that would help you numb your past? For example, alcohol, prescription drugs, excessive planning to keep yourself busy so your mind doesn't catch up with you, or hiding from yourself and from others so they don't know what you actually think of yourself. So the world doesn't find out who you actually are. If so, you're not alone. You're driven by and motivated by the things you fear and the things that have affected you tremendously. It's okay; we all need somewhere to start. It may be where we are now, but it won't be the same where we're going. There are those out there who can show a more excellent way, and now that we've come to terms with ourselves, we're happy to receive a new process and replace the one that has gotten us this far. It might not have been all bad, but mediocre is not the life that we are called to live. We just need a little hope to get us going.

Needing Hope

When you're stuck with yourself, who is there to lead you? Now I'm fifteen, staring out into the world with the classic excitement of marriage or, should I say, the fairytale of marriage. Because, if I'm being honest, I had no examples of what a good marriage looked like. I was a few years away from legally being allowed to drive or drink. Not that I wanted to drink anyway because I'd witnessed its abuse in my past. In the traditional sense, I was far from being an adult. So, what is a fifteen-year-old to do to accelerate their adulthood? You guessed it. I looked down and saw my belly, pregnant with my first son. He joined the world before my sixteenth birthday. While others were getting ready for prom and homecoming, I was getting ready for a baby.

As much of a joyful time as it was, Douglas's presence added extra responsibility. Another person to care for meant more emotional weight on top of my confused, fractured soul. Of course, when we got the invitation to pull up our bootstraps and get to work, we did just that. My husband Doug went right to work. He brought such stability to my life that I had never experienced. He was raised in a good Christian home. After we got married, I remember how I thought every bathroom had Playboy magazines in it because It was so normal for me to see naked women on display in ours. But to my surprise, they did not. My father did not try to hide his magazines like I think most men do. Nope, he left them open for anyone and all to see including my mother. There wasn't anything normal about that. I can only imagine how my mother must have felt seeing those images in her own home.

Unsurprisingly, when Douglas was six months old, Doug and I wanted to get a divorce. We had one of a thousand arguments that day; I remember it as if it were yesterday. We looked up a random attorney in the phone book, swung by their office to break this thing up and go our separate ways, and there was a Post-It note on the door. It said sorry, the office is closed due to unexpected events. So we got back in the car, went home, and continued working on our relationship. The thing that drove me inside to reset every six months was still there. And let's be honest, life was hard; the bills didn't stop when you fed three people, and we were so young. Normally, people have time to work through some of their problems when they first get together, before marriage. Because we got married so young, we worked on all of our problems with each other, which didn't make it easy, especially when you do not know how to communicate effectively during the foundational parts of a marriage. There were a few things that we were working toward. We were doing everything we could to keep our marriage together after we decided to continue to work on it. The climb was at times unbearable. And I would be lying if I said I didn't question so many times if it was worth it.

Also, I knew I was never going to be relying on any government support. For anything! This was a hardcore rule that I had because I visibly remembered the shame on my mother's face every time she used food stamps. I can still see it to this day. I knew I would never, ever do that. This was my opinion, and because I felt so much other shame, it felt compounding. Of course, if others require assistance, then it's there and I pass no judgment whatsoever. So, I vowed to myself that I'd prefer to work ten jobs than rely on a single cent from the government. It became my bond.

In addition to not relying on any handouts, we really wanted to buy a house. I just felt it would bring so much more stability if we could give Douglas a home to live in. We were renting at the time and everything inside of me wanted to give Douglas his own room that he could keep so he would feel stable. I wanted him to have the childhood that I never had. So, we saved up enough money to buy our first house when I was seventeen. The mortgage was $367 per month. My husband and I worked our butts off to ensure we had enough money. I started babysitting and cleaning libraries with my mother-in-law at fifteen, until I picked up a job as a waitress. I would work the split shift. I would go in at ten a.m., get off at 2:30 p.m., and then return for the evening shift after being home for a few hours. Thankfully, my mother-in-law was there to watch Douglas while I worked. My husband and I were in the grind of family duty. We would pass each other as he got off work and I went back in on the split shift. We were both just trying to get by.

Feeling Stuck

As I built my family, I realized every area of myself that was not developed and perfected would show itself. My flaws, lack of identity, insecurities, and shame kept me from moving forward in life. Of course, I became a highly functioning mom and wife and kept my inner world private; no one knew. Have you ever known a highly functioning alcoholic who can work a forty-hour work week, come home everyday pounding down the emotion with every drink until they pass out, yet wake up every morning for work? I do. That was my step-grandfather. Isn't that what we all do? We bottle it in and make sure that the lid is squeezed on tight, and we hope and pray we don't have an explosion in front of people we care about. Although I wasn't an alcoholic, I was hiding secrets of my childhood and past.

More often than not, we reveal our flaws to our family consistently. It's like the world put them in a place to iron them out with us. Ooh, like when they say the wrong things, it triggers us. My trigger was always to shut down completely. With each trigger I had, I became more aware of how broken I truly was. Perhaps you're not into the blaming as many are. If not, then you self-criticize. You're mindfully aware of your flaws because that inner voice always reminds you. You know how Broken you are and how messed up your past is. Sometimes, we're scared that people might discover who we are and then choose not to love us. So, we convinced ourselves that we need to put on a show and provide them with half-truths so they don't misunderstand the characterization we would like to portray.

We know this critical voice too well. As a matter of fact, it's the only voice we hear. It doesn't matter what other people tell us. The voice that screams the loudest is always in between our ears. Those demons never stop professing our failures to us. If only we could find some sense of freedom and move on from the lies that we've told ourselves and that we believed. We work so hard to build a polished external life so that people can be happy with us and we can look accomplished, but we know how messy things are in our minds. We know how convoluted our emotions are and our selves are in the world that we live in. We're confused and lost. We look for things to do because it fills up the space. It fills the void we have inside.

Anytime the emptiness is felt, we convince ourselves to do something or go somewhere to solve it. It's only temporal.

Eventually, decades pass by, and we realize we haven't made any progress in our hearts. We don't feel any closer to who we could become. We don't feel and see that we're living through our true potential because we're unhappy with ourselves. Of course, we are critical of outcomes as we can always do better. We've let our past shape our future and we are no better than a wandering star. There's no place we call home inside or where we find value and meaning. Of course, we have a physical home. I'm not talking about that; I'm talking about a source of affection that goes beyond ourselves. A source of hope that goes beyond the feelings we can drum up before breakfast. Surely, there's something greater than we can pull from to access our purpose and meaning. Surely, there's more to this life. Surely, there's a way out to find my identity instead of this mud pit I've created. I knew after years of surviving that I needed hope, and I did not know my whole life was about to change.

On the Porch One Day

When I was twenty-three, we went on a trip to visit my grandpa in Tennessee. He was not your typical grandpa. We didn't have much of a relationship growing up, but I knew he was a preacher, wore bib overalls, and played the guitar. We went there Labor Day weekend 1996. The drive wasn't too far, so we made it work. The whole family went. By this time, I had had our daughter, Kristie. We stayed a few days and enjoyed the different scenery, company, and my step-grandmother's sweet tea. The trip ended quickly. As we were on our way out on Sunday, my grandpa and I took a walk before we left. I don't remember anything of the conversation that day other than him saying, "I'm so glad you're saved." I looked at him and said, "Saved? I have no idea what you're talking about. What does that even mean?"

He said, "Oh my God, we have to talk." So, we went into his tiny camper. See, when my grandpa finally decided to permanently lay his stakes down in Tennessee, he was in his sixties; therefore, he was behind when it came to building roots and lived in a camper on some land. He also, like my father, was a gypsy soul who pulled his stakes up often. As he asked me if I knew anything about salvation, I said NO, I knew nothing. He said, "Do you believe in Jesus Christ?" So, here was a man I hardly knew speaking to me in a foreign language and using words I did not know. I had never been taken to church, much less learned the church's vocabulary. He said, "Let me tell you a story."

As he sat across from me on that day, he told me about Jesus. He told me that Jesus came on the earth and died for me. He told me how they beat him beyond recognition and hung him on the cross, and placed a crown of thorns on his head. He shared with me the nails that went into Jesus's hands and feet and how blood came out of his side when they pierced him with the spear. He told me that the blood of Jesus was shed so that I could be saved. I believe my grandpa spoke with such deep conviction because of his past and the amount of mercy and grace that he'd found from the God he had served his whole life. You see, my grandpa loved Jesus, the road, and women. He learned early on that temptation can walk right into the church with red high heels on, and if he wasn't guarded, he would fall hook, line, and unfortunately for him, sinker. You see, my grandpa left my grandma for another woman when my father was a young boy. My grandma was very sick at the time when my grandpa left her. My father said he took her back to Ohio, dumped her off like a piece of trash on the side of the road, and left them in the dust. The pattern was the same as my father's.

Even though I knew all that about the man I called Grandpa, who was sitting across from me, something about the kindness in his voice grabbed my attention as he shared the Life of Christ with me. I held on to every word he spoke. Tears fell like buckets from my eyes as my heart came alive. My grandpa then walked me through a repentance prayer and a prayer to invite God into my heart and life. I did just that. It was like standing under a waterfall; I felt, somehow, cleaned and renewed. I met the Redeemer, who gave me deep, eternal hope, something I'd never felt before.

My grandpa said, "Now, you have to go tell somebody. That's the only way it sticks. You got to tell somebody." I was happy, too. I went down to my uncle's and told his wife, Lisa. There was no question that I was a different person walking out of that little camper. When it happened, I didn't have any words to describe it. But now, I knew I had walked out of the darkness the moment I'd accepted Jesus into my life. I knew something was different. My whole life just changed in a matter of minutes. I finally met the one I dreamed of, longed for, and needed so much.

Finally, I had someone who could relate to my confusion, pain, and past. I found the author of Love. He was so gentle and sweet to my heart; He could have easily picked me apart because of my sin, but instead, He surrounded me with His love. That was the first time I could say I experienced true Joy. Instantly, my heart changed that day, and my mind was slowly changing with it. I finally felt like I was on the right path to who I was called to be. I felt like I could breathe again.

I was in shock and awe. The more I considered the possibilities of what took place, the more I realized what I was missing the whole time. I had a swirl of emotions from the great promises that came with Jesus and letting go of my past. I knew he was the one I was missing, so I was filled with tremendous joy and excitement while also being reminded of how much I thought of myself. I knew I had a lot of work to do in sorting out my own thoughts and feelings, but now I had someone to do that with me. I had someone who had all the answers. I knew that he cared for my needs. This led me down a beautiful season of falling in love with Jesus.

Mary

Mary, the mother of Jesus, had a somewhat different path. She was set apart and chosen by God for the purpose and plan my God had for her from the very beginning. She was qualified because of her lineage and because of her heart. The Bible says that she followed all of the statutes of the Lord, and when God looked down upon the Earth, He found that she was Worthy. When the angel Gabriel told her that she would bear a son and his name would be Jesus, she asked the question that all of us would ask: "How?" Perhaps her faith had already led her to this moment where she was asking how she wanted to get right into her assignment instead of doubting God's plans for her. She said, "Be it unto me according to your word." Wow! She was a woman of faith. She had proven herself to be a willing vessel for God. It seems fitting that she found herself thirty years later at a wedding with her son, Jesus.

Now, the wedding traditions were quite extensive back then. It was customary for the bride and groom to prepare enough wine for everyone. They had plenty of time to prepare to ensure everything was there before the wedding. At this wedding, a time came when Mary was made aware that they had run out of wine. Jesus was sitting there with his disciples, enjoying himself, and Mary said, "They have no more wine." "Woman, why do you involve me?" Jesus replied. "My hour has not yet come." His mother told the servants, "Do whatever he tells you."

This may seem confusing for some because, up until this point, Jesus had not worked any miracles. He had been around Mary for the last thirty years, though. On the third day of this wedding, the bride and the groom ran out of wine. What a shameful experience. They didn't plan and prepare properly for the wedding. Some would have said that it was ruined because of this. Now, Mary, being the mother of Jesus, making sure that everyone has their wine, brought this matter to the Lord. Can you imagine? She had the faith and unction to turn to Jesus, look Him in the eyes, and say they had no more wine. She probably gave Him one of those motherly power pauses. And in that moment, Jesus replied and said, "Woman, why do you involve me? My hour has not yet come."

Well, if you remember, when Jesus first experienced John the Baptist while also in the womb, Elizabeth was filled with the spirit of God, and Mary prophesied who Jesus would become even before he was born. Mary was filled with the spirit of God, and she sang a song about Jesus.

And Mary said, My soul glorifies the Lord, and my spirit rejoices in God my Savior, for he has been mindful of the humble state of his servant. From now on, all generations will call me blessed, for the Mighty One has done great things for me—holy is his name. His mercy extends to those who fear him, from generation to generation. He has performed mighty deeds with his arm; he has scattered those who are proud in their inmost thoughts. He has brought down rulers from their thrones but has lifted up the humble. He has filled the hungry with good things but has sent the rich away empty. He has helped his servant Israel, remembering to be merciful to Abraham and his descendants forever, just as he promised our ancestors." (Luke 1:46-55)

She was saying and professing things that she had not yet even seen in the flesh. The nature of God had been revealed to her by the Holy Spirit. Her faith was abounding. She sang of his extended mercy and his compassion. She sang of his mighty Deeds with his stretched-out arm and his magnificent Kingdom. All of these things were placed there by God.

Now, can you imagine having the spirit of God inside of you professing the nature of Jesus? And you are waiting for it to come to pass. Thirty years of waiting. Thirty years of sitting across from him at dinner, wondering if today is the day. So, we return to the wedding. Mary went over to Jesus and said they had no more wine. Jesus replied that his hour had not yet come. Then Mary did something remarkable. She called on the Father, moved in faith, looked to his servants, and said, "Do whatever he tells you to do." Ahh! It was almost as if she couldn't take one more minute without Jesus revealing himself to the world. Can you imagine the look on the disciples' faces when they realized that Mary's faith had just moved Jesus into his miraculous season?

Jesus was moved, and he assisted in saving the wedding by making more wine. *Nearby stood six stone water jars, the kind used by the Jews for ceremonial washing, each holding from twenty to thirty gallons. Jesus said to the servants, "Fill the jars with water," so they filled them to the brim. Then he told them, "Now draw some out and take it to the master of the banquet." They did so, and the master of the banquet tasted the water that had been turned into wine. He did not realize where it had come from, though the servants who had drawn the water knew. Then he called the bridegroom aside and said, "Everyone brings out the choice wine first and then the cheaper wine after the guests have had too much to drink, but you have saved the best till now." (John 2:6-10)*

When you're filled with hope, faith comes easy. Mary showed us what a pure heart and a righteous mind do for the soul. She saw things in Jesus that changed her purpose and her daily realities. She was able to draw on him in times of need. She is an example of who we could become when we find God. The moment she made herself available to God, He showed Himself faithful and proved her faithfulness every day. She found Hope, and she never let Him go. Sure enough, after thirty years, hope showed his face.

Redeemer

A wandering soul is always looking for a redeemer, like a wandering star is looking for a path. Deep down inside, we need direction, or we will slowly erode into nonexistence. Who is there to lead us if we've only known ourselves? Perhaps we follow someone who's gone down the path before. Someone we find relatable in the trials and in the victories. They will be our guide and show us the way.

This was an all too familiar reality for Israel, the children of God. The Israelites frequently found themselves wandering in life, in the wilderness, into the land of nothingness. They frequently put themselves in harm's way. Sometimes, they held their faith for twenty minutes after hearing a word from their leader or God Himself. They loved messing up continuously. They had a knack for it. This made them the perfect case study.

It didn't matter how dramatic the miracles were or how loud God spoke from the sky; they found a way to turn their backs on Him quickly and in a unique fashion. One time, they were messing up so much that God established a framework of Commandments that they had to abide by in order to not mess up so much. While Moses was up on the mountain receiving instructions from God, all of God's children, Israel, were making a golden calf out of all their jewelry so they could worship it while Moses was away. Perhaps they could have taken a nap or done some laps around the mountain instead. No, they decided to worship their jewelry.

Regardless of the self-initiated trials and tribulations, they needed a lot of help. There was no way they would find a path that led them anywhere close to life and prosperity if they just kept doing the same things repeatedly. They needed a guide. They needed a redeemer. The Impossible standard of the Commandments brought forth a perfect blueprint for Jesus. No one could come in and fulfill every one of the 613 Commandments. At some point, somewhere, you would mess up. And somehow, those Ten Commandments were the summation of perfection. Only one was able to follow them perfectly, and his name is Jesus.

We Are Israel

We may not all be of Middle Eastern descent, but each and every one of us is Israel in this story. If we were to go on our merry ways, our great-grandparents and grandparents, our parents, and ourselves, we would all find a way to mess up our perfect realities. Some of what we experience is self-initiated, and sometimes we are in the wrong place at the wrong time. Whether we've received the inheritance of sin or we participate in it on a regular basis, we're no different. Like the Apostle Paul says, we do the thing we know we shouldn't do.

No one is exempt from this story. We all have a list of our frailties, faults, and sins that we've rehearsed in our minds. Depending on the culture you grew up in, you might also celebrate it. It doesn't take much for us to quickly put on our hat of negativity and confess every problem we see with ourselves. We wear our scars like badges of honor, depending on who we're with. It's who we become or who we would not become that we identify with. If we were left to our own devices for too long, then we would continue wandering into the wilderness of life.

At some point, the meaninglessness and the empty voids start to speak to us. Even they don't want us around. It's like we're a seed that's been baking in the Sun, and we're finally at the end when it starts to rain. The thing with seeds that's magical is they must die before they're able to produce new life. New life begins when our hearts ask for more than what we're currently experiencing. It's a spiritual inquiry not unto ourselves but unto something so much greater. We know there must be more to this and what we're currently living. What could possibly be the meaning of all this madness and suffering? Can I possibly live a better life than I'm saying now?

Our Revelation

Once we've reached the resolution in our mind or heart that our path is less fulfilling than what's possible for our soul, we know we've fallen short. This revelation is actually the beginning of progress. We've had the opportunity to succeed on our own until now, but here we are with all this baggage. No clear vision or direction on what to do and how to get rid of it. Even if we feel the Embrace of success, it's quickly engulfed by our inner turmoil. Oh, we try to shake the feeling as often and as long as possible, and we're at the end of our coping strategies. Sleeping aids, temporal short-term escapes, and loud music can no longer quiet the voices inside.

The voices aren't all lies. They tell us the truth about ourselves in addition to the exaggerated stories of our imagination and fears. We know they're true to some extent, so we hang on to them. They're justified in staying as a part of our identity because this is Who We Are. This is the person I am. How could I separate the good from the bad within myself? I don't have the power to do that. These are the conversations we have with ourselves. They are valid, and you alone cannot save yourself.

However, there is one who can save us from ourselves. See, before time began, God in heaven dreamed within Himself the world of free thinkers made in the image of Him. Such autonomy is guaranteed to fail because of choice. This required God to send His own son in the flesh to a world that was confused about her purpose and identity. The world testified to His coming for years before Christ's arrival because of the growing pains of persistent failure and sin. It was almost as if the world was unified in crying out for a savior.

Finally, a window of time opened, and Jesus revealed himself on the Earth. He was perfect in every aspect of the world. He perfectly fulfilled every jot and title of the law when no one else could. He introduced the world to love through a resounding acceptance of people that was beyond anything the world had ever seen up until that point. It was almost as if he knew exactly the world's potential while simultaneously understanding its frailties.

He spoke in parables and mysteries to those who were proud. For the simple and accepting, he spoke kind and beautiful things about the kingdom of God. He was the most relatable person who had ever walked the Earth while simultaneously not being a part of the world's systems and problems. Men from high societal positions offered him the spot in government and the ability to position himself to rule and reign on the Earth with them, but He rejected this because they didn't understand why he was there.

Jesus saw within himself the joy that was set before him, which was you and I and every person he encountered. He came to redeem us to the Father by positioning himself as the spotless lamb who was slain before the foundation of the world. The sins of every generation cried out to him, demanding an answer, and he was going to meet it. Jesus, as God, was going to lay down his life to become the ultimate sacrifice for humanity. He did just that; he gave himself over to his accusers, and they beat and tortured him to death.

The brutality of sin required death as its ultimate payment. Nothing else would satisfy its demands. If we were to hang on to our sin, it would be the end of us. For in it, we would find death and not life. Jesus knew this extremely well. The payment that he made on the cross was sufficient to satisfy the demands of sin. He took it upon himself to pay a price for a sin he had not committed. His payment was retroactive because he was God. He not only paid the price for everyone in the past but also for everyone who was yet to come.

The Redeemer

That day, when I gave my life to Christ, the realization that I was bought with a price is what changed everything for me. How was this payment sufficient for my insecurities and frailties in my life? It's because he rose from the dead. He didn't stay in the grave but rose from what bound him. Perfect in every way, tempted in everything, he paid the price for me and conquered sin and death. I realized that he not only died for me but also lived for me.

My Redeemer Lives and his name is Jesus. I couldn't get enough of Jesus the moment I got saved. No time lapsed from when we got home; I knew I had to find a church immediately. That following Sunday, I was in church and I went every single time they opened up the doors. Three times a week, my kids and I were there. I tried to soak it all in and embrace everything I could about Jesus. Every revelation changed my life because it allowed me to think outside of myself and accept a redeemer for my life.

How do I measure full redemption or at least try to? In my twenties and thirties, I was so engulfed in the shame of not graduating, becoming a teenage wife and mother, and leaving home at such a young age that redemption was a word I thought I was acquainted with and knew; however, I had no idea what the word meant until my late forties. Redemption is the action of regaining or gaining possession of something in exchange for payment or clearing a debt. The day Jesus died on that cross and rose again, a debt for my sin was paid in full. His work was made complete. Now, I have to accept that and integrate his completed work into my life.

The Bible says that I died with him, and I rose with him in the spiritual sense. It also says that I'm a new creation, something that has never been seen before on Earth. A redeemed person, perfected in the eyes of God because of Jesus's payment. Redemption means I did not have to work for it. All I had to do was understand and walk in it. Walk in freedom, freedom from the chains of shame. Even though I was a woman of faith, a woman of prayer, a woman of God's word for many years at this point in my life, I still did not fully walk in freedom. Suppose I had only understood this, my goodness, how things would have been entirely different. I would not have hidden behind the door of shame all those years. I would have embraced my identity fully, which goes back to my origin. My name. Mika. One who is like God.

You see, when I was born, my birth name was Teresa. A few days after my mother got home from the hospital, my grandmother, Mae, called her and said, "You have to change her name to Mika." So, that's what my mother did. I often look at the two birth certificates, two names, one of who I should have been and the other who I was destined to be. I stand in complete awe, knowing God's fingerprint was the signature on that document.

As my grandmother lay dying in the hospital, I had the privilege of leading her to Christ. Shortly after, she said a tall man with a long white coat came to her bedside and in his hand was a gold thread. She said she heard music and he placed the gold thread in her belly button. You see, she could hardly eat. The next day while I visited her in the hospital, she told me about it. I said, "Grandma, that was an angel who visited and fed you." A few days later, she died. Words fail me when it comes to describing the impact she had on my life. The same woman who said, "You have to change her name to Mika." My God, how deep is His love for us?

The enemy is a liar, a murderer of dreams, visions, and life. There is a story of full redemption in every woman who has stood fearlessly with the wind against her back, looking through life with a scratched lens. It took me five years to unpack all my childhood baggage, let God heal the deep wounds, and use my story for His glory. Do not get me wrong; it still stings, and at times, I have a lump in my throat. I often think back to the vision God gave me in 2022. I was in heavy prayer, and God showed me an old stone well; as I approached the well, I looked inside it, and a little girl was down at the bottom. God spoke so tenderly and said, "When you open your mouth to tell your story, you will throw the rope down to her, and she will climb out." My heart started pounding out of my chest as He spoke because as I looked inside the well, I knew the girl was me when I was six. She had been stuck there all those years. Not of her own doing like so many other women. At that moment, I realized that the first memory I have of my father was him leaving us on the porch when I was six and how that scarred me for life.

Jesus paid the price for you to walk in freedom, victory, and redemption. The road will not always be easy, but having God on your side will surely help. When you can fly without broken wings, that is the ultimate measure of complete redemption.

A Life Worth Living

For the first time in my life, I could breathe without the weight of shame. I was slowly removing the bricks one by one. I was free from the bondage of my past and every label that was given. I finally had permission to dream again and fill my heart with hope and a vision for my life so I could walk into my true purpose and calling. I knew I was just beginning this new journey, and I was so optimistic about where it could take me because my guide was wonderful and kind. Jesus is compassionate, loving, and very understanding. He's also very relatable and can speak to my intricacies like no one else. We are friends and I long to talk with him daily.

I knew my new life was going to take some getting used to. Yesterday, I was a different person than I am today. I knew I had to learn how to accept my salvation daily in my thoughts and heart so I could migrate my lifestyle into something more lifegiving for myself and my family. My spirit was saved yesterday, but my mind hadn't been saved yet. I knew that process would take some time, but I was open to the journey because God is faithful.

Do you know how we can exist and not really live our lives? Whether we're surviving or just trying to fill the void of the empty space, living is not truly living unless we're redeemed. Why redemption? What does it even matter? Simply put, it gives our life meaning. What are you living for? Are you living for yourself or for someone else? Perhaps you cannot see a generation in a legacy that is yours to start.

Christ's redemptive work is pivotal because it unlocks the Redemptive purpose. If we have a season, moment, or innocence lost because of sin or recklessness, we can lean on a redemptive purpose to redeem that time for us. It helps us reset and compensate for lost feelings, life, freedoms, and purpose. When he is a redeemer at work in our lives, we can look at our past with redemption, allowing us to create a Bedrock of meaning so our lives can be used for good and it's not all lost.

Ruth's Redemptive Purpose

Ruth is a perfect example of redemptive purpose. She marries a man who dies, and she becomes a childless widow who chooses to accompany her mother-in-law, Naomi, to Judah. Naomi wasn't too interested in having Ruth around, but her persistence paid off. Ruth pledged her undying loyalty to Naomi, her people, and her God, Yahweh. This brought Ruth on an Epic Journey where she disavowed her former identity and renounced her former religious affiliations. She was shedding her old skin so she could walk into something new. Sound familiar?

One day, she was taking the initiative to find food, and by chance, she came to the field of a prosperous man named Boaz. Tradition has it that 10 percent of the crops on the street were accessible to those in need. Boaz, being a very prosperous man, allowed Ruth to glean in the field. He allowed her to see her true potential and what she had access to. Boaz invoked a blessing upon her from Yahweh, under whose protective wings she had taken Refuge.

Ruth agreed to marry the man who had it all, Boaz. He invited her up under the covers after they celebrated the harvest, and they went to sleep. Ruth asked for his cover, and Boaz found her a worthy woman. The kinsman redeemer found her worthy in his sight.

We may find ourselves like Ruth at the beginning, where we set on a course and make commitments that fail us. When we have sight of hope and promise, and we pursue it with everything we've got, it will lead us to a kinsman redeemer like Boaz. Ruth married the one who had it all when she was just gleaning on the edge of the field. Our curiosity about Christ is paralleled here in the kinsman redeemer. As we consider Christ to be our ultimate Redeemer, once we're done gleaning on the edge of the field, he'll invite us into a deeper and more profound relationship.

When God Calls Us

∞⊂∞⊃∞⊂∞⊃∞⊂∞⊃∞⊂∞⊃∞

When God calls from the heavens, some people say it thunders. They hear clanging and banging from the sky like lightning cracking through the clouds. Others say they hear a kind voice, calling them as a father calls their child unto himself. Why does one person hear a soothing voice from their Father and another hears a destructive noise from the sky? It's simple. The choice may seem to be ours, but it's not. Those who have tuned their hearing to listen to the Father's soothing voice from above vs. those who hear banging and clashing, in the latter instance, their heart is not attuned to His voice. This is to protect them in their position. His voice is not clear to them, regardless of the case—indifference, turning away, sinfulness, or circumstance. This is but a gift for those who cannot bear it. If His voice were clear to them while they continued to run away, then His voice would crush them. The purity with which He speaks displaces Darkness and Evil. One could not remain with a hardened heart while the Lord professes over them. This is why He chooses us first. What do I mean when I say He chooses us first?

The heavens and the Earth are His, along with everything within it. His words stretch the sky from east to west, and He sees the past, present, and future all at once. In Him, nothing is hidden, and therefore, nothing surprises Him. So, within the constraints of time, He looks at our hearts and says that He has chosen us. This happens at the Proper time. When He calls us, He knows we're ready to receive Him. He is merciful and would not allow us to endure something we could not bear. But when the time is right, He calls us out of darkness and into His marvelous Light because He knows we're ready. And therefore, whether it's a moment before our choice to pursue Him and accept Him or it's an entire eternity before, He chooses us first. He surely had more time to consider a matter than we did, and therefore, in His perfection, we will accept the fact that we are chosen not of our own volition but through His tender mercies and perfect timing.

For years, I grew up in my own world of thought, trying to survive while listening to the clanging, banging noises from above. I remember driving home from work, trapped in my own thoughts. I would think to myself, what would happen if I wrapped this car around that telephone pole over there? Would anybody care? I know people say they love me, but I'm tormented inside. What if it all ended right now? What would actually happen? Who would care? Even though I was married, I had kids. There was no hope I could find inside. I felt that hopelessness all the time.

I always felt so tired of trying to make sure that nobody knew about my past or how I grew up because they would label me. They would think differently of me for not graduating high school like everybody else did. They would think differently of me for sleeping in a tent when I was younger instead of having a home like everybody else did. They'd call me ignorant and stupid, someone with no sense of purpose and no life. Through all of the clanging and banging of noises coming from above, I couldn't hear anything good about myself or about my future because the inner voice was so strong.

Nothing would transpire if I prayed unto myself or to another because I could only hear thunder from above. It was all noise. Nothing made sense; no clear answer or direction was given until my heart was ready and I accepted His mercy that day as I looked across the table at my grandfather. I no longer heard the inaudible noise but the voice of Our Father in heaven.

The clarity with which He spoke to my heart that day pierced every veil and defense that I had built through the years. I always thought that I chose Him, but the more I got to know Him, the more I realized that He, in fact, chose me. I was the joy that was set before Him that He would endure the cross. He was not about to waste His investment in me by simply sealing me unto the day of redemption and leaving me in my mess. He gave me an invitation to my transformation, which He calls salvation. It is a process for which we're called that rids us of our former selves and brings us into our redemptive state.

As difficult as it may sound, His timing was perfect. It's easy to question the things that we don't know and don't understand. One could fill a mountain up with "whys." Why didn't you call me out of the darkness sooner? Why didn't you stop the harm from being done? Why did you allow such evil things to happen to me? We may have many understandably valid questions when we start to gain clarity as to who He is to us. We're trying to sort out our lives and understand what transpired and why. We want to test the bounds of His faithfulness and His truth. We want to be reassured in our convictions and faith. For most people, we want to receive comfort and assurance that our trials and tribulations were not in vain and that they are understood.

As we learn our rightful place in Him as the Redeemer, we will begin to understand the context in which He created us. We were born into a world of fully empowered, free-willed individuals who are actively participating in good and evil simultaneously. Some see it fit to deploy and pursue the good in the world, and others imagine and create evil scenarios for themselves and everyone around them based on the God-given ability to self-govern. This means everything that they do affects all of us because of our relationship and proximity to one another. This ultimate power of self-governing has its downsides when it's abused; people are mistreated, taken advantage of, and even worse. Only an evil imagination can come up with the kinds of terror that people have been put through over the decades and continue to be put through. As you can work out, unwinding such events in our minds and hearts will take some time.

The Call

If we are prisoners of our own making and one comes to pay the debts we owe to set us free, we are indeed free. We are redeemed as we leave the prison that day, but has the prison left us? Meeting the Redeemer is an invitation for us to be called out of darkness into light. This invitation indeed transforms us as it has cleared our debts and set us free, but we are still bound by the past that we once lived and the emotions and thoughts that got us there. This requires a process in which we die daily to ourselves so that we may accept a new profound grace in the morning. We are called to cast away the former things to accept the new vessel God has called us to.

This is the process of walking out our salvation and perfecting our faith. It is not a question of whether or not God's work for us was enough. That matter is not up for debate. His work is finished and will always be complete and profound. The matter that is up for debate is our implementation of His completed work in our lives. Upon initial introduction, we receive an invitation at the door of a new life. This life we gladly accept because it sets us free. Now, it is up to us to implement His transformative grace and the gifts from above to rid our minds, hearts, and emotions of all that keep us back from becoming what He has intended for us to be.

The calling is not what it may seem. When we have a call, we pick up our phones, communicate, and end the call. When God gives us a calling, it is a lifelong journey. Why would it be so long, one might ask? It's because the greatest thing that we can do in our lives is to be Unbound by the former things that were not from Him and to be free to choose Him and His reward. Where do we go with this calling? The destination we seek is Him. He is our goal; He is our reward. We do not put our faith in corruptible things that will be gone tomorrow. We put our faith in our Creator because He has led us out of Egypt and paid our debts.

Lydia's Call

Paul and Silas from the New Testament were traveling to Philippi. They stopped to speak to a woman who was at a place of Prayer. One of those listening was Lydia from the city of Thyatira. She was a businesswoman and a dealer of purple cloth. The Bible calls her a worshiper of God. At the time of Paul's speaking, the Bible says that Lydia's heart opened up. The Bible goes on to say that the Lord opened up her heart to respond to Paul's message. As Paul spoke, she heard the Father's voice, and the Lord opened her heart. It was the perfect time for Lydia. She and the other members of her household became baptized and invited Paul and Silas back to her house to stay.

She's on record for being one of the first converts of Europe to the Christian faith. She could be seen in the same light as Mary, who was going about her life doing what she knew how to do, and then God called her. How many others received the same invitation that day and didn't pick up the phone to answer? How many others did Paul and Silas speak to on their Journeys who denied the call of God? Lydia's heart was ready; therefore, the Lord responded and opened her heart to accept Him. What a precious and beautiful thing for God to take residency in us and invest His precious presence in our lives. Lydia did the most expected thing next: she became baptized and wanted to learn more. One thing that's guaranteed if you want to spend more time with someone is you give them a place to stay. Imagine the conversations they had about what God has done.

Sense of Structure

I, too, heard the call of God for my life, just as Lydia did. My acceptance of Christ into my life brought an instant sense of structure that I so desperately needed. The weight that I was feeling my entire life was gone instantly. I went home that day and knew I had to find a church to teach me and help me make sense of everything. Most importantly, I needed a structure outside of myself to help facilitate the change. I found a little Baptist Church, and that's where I decided to go. I fell in love with everything they were doing. I just wanted to be involved. I signed up for everything, and I volunteered for everything. I just wanted to be available. I love being a part of this new life.

We used to sing from the little blue Hymnal books old songs that you don't hear anymore. It was a tiny little Country Church that had services on Sunday and Wednesday, with two services on Sunday. Anytime those doors were open, me and my kids were there; they were three and seven at the time. My kids didn't have a choice. They were going. I knew deep down inside it was better for them to go to church than for them to have the childhood that I had. So, they were going to church.

My husband didn't catch on to the Christian thing as fast as I did because of his past disappointments. He grew up in the church and had some bitter moments that were hard to overcome. He saw the fake parts of the church, leaving you unsettled with a bitter and uneasy taste in your mouth. How can one human behave with great evil and harm and yet call themselves a child of God? His experience with Christians was sometimes perplexing, as it is for all of us. Plenty of double-mindedness was going on, and it was off-putting, to say the least. He went sometimes but considered it overkill. In my mind, the void of not having God was so great that it felt like every time I attended church and participated in anything surrounding God, it was slowly but surely filling me up.

It was very cold that day in November. I believe it was snowing, and I decided to get baptized in the Ohio river. Of course, it was freezing, but it was worth it. I sought after Jesus as much as I could with like-minded people. My kids loved it, too, but I do remember when my son turned sixteen, I had to start dragging him to church. I would tell him that as long as you're alive and under my roof, you're going to church. Maybe my approach was radical, maybe not, all I knew was they were going to church with me. Period. I was learning a new way to live and getting to know my Father in heaven. Things truly began to change for me when I saw things for the first time through His eyes.

Through His Eyes

I started to learn ways to perceive my life and past through His eyes instead of my own. This was not some trickery. It was a matter of a healthy vs. unhealthy perspective. My ability to perceive what was true amid my confusion was limited, and His perspective was unlimited. One of the first things we all learn as we begin to accept Him is redemption and forgiveness and how they're available to us today. This gave me the ability to perceive my past through a different lens. A lens that is washed in the goodness of God vs. negativity. It showed me the beautiful parts of my past as a way to perceive and see the world anew.

As I look back, I can see the redemptive parts of my life for the first time. I could see my son, daughter, and husband and the joy they brought me. As weird as it may seem, my husband was the knight in shining armor for me this whole time. In a sense, he rescued me from a broken place and gave me a good life. One night while I was by myself on my way home from church, after my kids were grown and on their own, I found myself thinking about my life. Things like marrying so young and never experiencing all the things most people have experienced. Remember, I met Doug at thirteen. I never dated, I never went to football games, I never went to dances, never knew the excitement of driver's ed and getting your license. None of that was my reality. I'll never forget what happened next. God spoke so clearly to me and said, "Mika, you would have been an alcoholic. He saved you." I almost had to pull over to the side of the road because the tears wouldn't stop coming. That settled it once and for all. I knew with certainty my husband was indeed my guiding light, and although we had to fight through hell and back to keep our marriage, and many said we wouldn't last six months because of how young we were, he rose to the occasion and provided a safety net for me.

He started working for the school district when I got pregnant with our son, Douglas, and continued working for them as the head maintenance guy for thirty years. He was able to retire from that position at the age of fifty. His consistency gave us the ability to move into our home so quickly. It was a nice home around a thousand square feet; it wasn't a shack, but it wasn't a mansion either. We just wanted to make sure that Douglas had a place that he called home.

After my father left us, my parents got a divorce and my dad got married again to a woman who lived in Houston, Texas. She had three kids, and she was less than happy that he had three kids. We went one time to visit in the summer and while my father was gone for the day, she locked me and my siblings outside for the entire day. While her kids sat inside in the air conditioning, we were so hot sitting on the porch. Now, when my mother found this out, she was not happy and she demanded my father bring us home. Well, he brought us home and never left.

I'm not sure exactly how that happened, but perhaps it was her faithful persistence, not moving on, and not giving up on him. She was, in fact, the anchor for my father, and he came back. Isn't it amazing that the unmovable thing is what we desire the most? Perhaps my mom's faithfulness was what was unmovable for him. My father divorced his wife and remarried my mother, but his old ways were the same. The only thing that changed was he was a few years older.

When redemption and forgiveness start to set in, your belief system about your situation changes. It's like you see it from a totally different elevation or angle. Before, you were three inches away from your problem, and now you're twenty feet away from your problem. In light of God's forgiveness, grace, and mercy, this context gives us a more complete picture of our past trials and tribulations. Without God, we perpetuate and magnify our belief systems and internal negativity biases when we stare at our past. When we perceive our past Through The Eyes of God, we see redemption, hope, and promise. This is the beginning of change, to see things differently. The word "repentance" means to think differently or change your mind. This is what I was going through at the beginning of my salvation. I was starting to change my mind about things and adopt His thoughts for me instead of my thoughts for myself. Yet, I still saw my name hanging on a Christmas tree in the mall. My mother would put our name in for someone to adopt us for Christmas. Her intentions were the purest, and she did not want us kids to be without Christmas presents, but when you see your name hanging there, it does something internally to you.

As I started to see the world through His eyes, I could finally begin the healing journey. How could healing commence without a fresh perspective with a new desired outcome? Once I could embody His intent for my well-being, I could finally call upon Him to help me see things the way I should see them. This was an ultimate invitation to see the world through His eyes, a world in which I could finally evaluate my past slowly, thoroughly, and completely. It was most definitely the beginning of a very long season of healing.

Purge the Dark Shadows

There are only five recorded women in the genealogy of Jesus Christ in the Book of Matthew. Each one tells their own unique story. Historically, genealogies would refer to the man and not the woman, and so these are interesting and informative stories that might lend us great insight. Tamar is the first of those mentioned. Her story has many twists and turns, so bear with the explanation because it will provide us with beautiful insight. Her story begins with Judah. Judah met the daughter of a Canaanite man and had two kids with her. His first son was Er and the second was Onan. It came time to find a wife for Er, so Tamar was given to him.

The Lord considered Er as wicked, and the Lord put him to death. So Judah told his second son to go have a child with Tamar so she could conceive and he could fulfill his duty to her as a brother-in-law to raise up offspring for his brother. Onan slept with her but never impregnated her intentionally because of selfish reasons. The Lord considered this before his sight and found it wicked, so God also put him to death.

Judah then considered Tamar as some broken, cursed vessel. He told her to go and live in the back house and wait for another son to grow up, even though he had no intention of giving his young son over to her. The Bible says that Judah thought his young son might die too, just as his brothers had, so Tamar was destined to be a widow for the rest of her life.

After a long while, Judah's wife passed away. Tamar changed from her widow's clothes, covered herself with a veil to disguise herself, and positioned herself at the entrance of the road. When Judah saw her, he thought that she was a prostitute, for she had covered her face. Not realizing that she was his daughter-in-law, he went over to her and said, "Come now, let me sleep with you." Tamar said, "What will you give me in return?" Judah said that he would send a young goat from his flock. She then asked for him to pledge something until the young goat arrived. Judah said, "What pledge should I give you?" This was when she took the seal, its cord, and the staff in his hand.

Judah sent a young goat sometime later to fulfill his pledge and receive his seal, cord, and staff back, but no one was there. Three months later, Tamar was showing and was said to be guilty of prostitution, which would have broken her oath and promise to the family. Judah commanded her to come out and for her to be burned to death. And as she was brought out, she sent a message to her father-in-law Judah. She said, "I'm pregnant by the man who owns these." She was referring to the seal, the cord, and the staff in her hand. She asked Judah if he recognized them. Judah did and said she was more righteous than him, since he wouldn't give her his third son. Tamar gave birth to twins Perez and Zerah.

Finding Her Place

Imagine being selected to be a part of the genealogy of Jesus Christ from God's perspective. The selection from Judah that we read about today was essentially the selection from God at the time because His seed that was to be continued was the story that God wanted us to know about. Judah goes off and has two kids with a Canaanite man's daughter. Both of them end up either being Wicked or committing Wicked acts in the sight of God, and God decides to remove them from the equation. This may be hard for some to comprehend, given the Old Testament drama that tends to convey extreme outcomes, but we need to know that God has a story that He wants to tell. He has a genealogy that is of absolute importance to Him. Also, in God's perspective, the better thing to do was to remove the wickedness and place someone else in the position for righteousness to be fulfilled. Mind you, all of this was going on without the Redemptive blood of Jesus and, therefore, any actions brought about the severity of the law. So, let's hold our judgment for the actions of God in this situation because He was rightfully removing wickedness from His genealogy.

Now, Tamar was just a vessel who was found worthy. Much like Mary was the mother of Jesus, God selected her because of who she was, so she was given her hand in marriage to bear one of Jesus's ancestors, but it turns out she married someone Wicked. Then, in succession, she was to bear the child of her first husband's brother because the Legacy and inheritance were of utmost importance. He, too, turned out to be Wicked. So, now Tamar was sent off to be a widow and die alone in the back house, never to return to society or participate in other relationships. The thing that happened to her wasn't necessarily her fault. She did nothing to deserve this, even though she found herself in a very perplexing situation. She was unable to fulfill her destiny due to the wickedness of others.

Imagine the emotional roller coaster she must've experienced. Imagine the blame and introspection that she could test within herself about her plight in life. Here she was, so capable, so willing, yet those around her restrained her purpose in life. Imagine the bitterness and resentment she had to fight off continuously as she sat back, knowing that she could not move forward and she couldn't redo anything in her past. What was she left to do? She must have gone through a time of purging and healing in order to bring herself enough courage to think creatively about her next steps.

The biblical account of her story is quite linear in its chronological progression, but imagine every single day having to fight off the deep, dark pits of negative emotion and keep her heart pure so that God would one day do something and open up an opportunity for her. Only heaven knows how many days she worked on herself before God so that she could be a willing vessel ready to receive what God had for her. In a beautiful progression, she comes up with a very interesting scenario in which she presents herself to the man whose seed God was destined to give her. In addition to his seed being given to her as it was intended originally through his son, he also gave her the seal, the cord, and the staff. These weren't random trinkets that he carried along. They were essentially the credit card, the personal seal of authority, and access to Judah's succession line. She was given the seed and the keys to his household. Most beautifully, God gave her twins to replace the wicked two. And out of her womb came the next child who would be in the succession of Jesus Christ.

Her story embodies the literal and spiritual principles of the promise of God and the promise of hope. Tamar is said to be more righteous than Judah out of his own mouth, which is a testament to her heart and why God chose her. Unfortunately, the situation played out in a way where even though she was righteous, she still went through a tremendous amount of disappointment, confusion, and mistreatment. She was accused of being broken and cursed. To us, we know God's intent, but to Judah, he thought she was the problem. Judah might not have seen the wickedness in his kid's Hearts as God did. She was essentially thrown to the wayside to waste away her years in the back house, and then, on top of that, she was accused of breaking the oath that she had made to the family.

She had to continually purge her heart and keep it pure before

God so that she could do everything God intended for her to do. Ultimately, she's the hero God wanted us to know about. Perhaps there are many others like her, but what made her so special was that she was willing to work through her thoughts, emotions, and behaviors to remain righteous in the sight of God.

40 Years Later

About a year after I got saved, I started a cleaning business. I had been a waitress at a high-end restaurant for several years. I waited on a couple frequently and grew to love them. One night, the woman, Noreen, asked me a question: "Would you be interested in cleaning on the side?" I immediately responded, "YES!"

See, God had already been nudging me to quit. I would tell Doug, "I feel God wants me to leave," but he would say, "Mika, you can't, we need the income." So, that night, I knew God sent the answer right to me in the form of cleaning.

I turned in my two weeks' notice before my shift was over. I went home and started crying, telling Doug I had turned my notice in. I was nervous about the unknown. He said, "I sure hope you know what you're doing." I said, "I do not, but I know enough to know this is the direction God is leading me." Here I was, a twenty-four-year-old young girl who had never once been taken to church, new to the Christian faith, yet I knew God was calling me. Over time, I grew this business quite well, and it has provided a great living for my family and has gone to generate millions in revenue.

It is the reason my husband got to retire at fifty and not have to worry. I've kept this going for the last several decades, and what a blessing it has been. All by saying one word: "YES." Now, my daughter, son, and their spouses are running the family business day-to-day operations, which has given me the freedom to pursue my desires.

In May of 2017, I was speaking at a conference. There was a man visiting from Nigeria in the crowd. After the service was over, he came up to me and asked if he could pray over me. I said, of course. While praying, he said, "Woman of God, doors will open to you, and you will never have to open them yourself." Well, I left there and knew God was doing something big in my life. Shortly after that, in early 2018, I felt God calling me to coach other businesses and become certified. I quickly had a list of thirty-three people from all over the U.S. who wanted help with their businesses. I was very excited to jump into this because I knew it was what I was supposed to do for my next season. I was traveling most of 2019–2021 all over the map and loved it.

By this time, Doug and I had started a real estate investing business and had properties in three different states. We take Proverbs 13:22 as gospel and believe in leaving our kids and grandkids something they can multiply. In 2021, I felt getting my real estate license would help me learn more about the real estate business. I enrolled in real estate school and passed all the classes. Then came the time to fill out the application to take my state exam. When I was reading the application, my heart stopped and tears welled up so big in my eyes you could have felt their weight as they fell on my counter. I called my kids to come over. They knew something was wrong. I showed the application to them and said, "Read that," as I pointed to the underlined question. What year did you graduate? That was the weighty question.

When I became certified in coaching on the application, the question was asked, but the director asked me to write a summary of my life and business experiences, and they would decide from there. But this was the state of Ohio, and there was no way a letter would do. My son said, "Just put the year you would have graduated; they will never ask for proof." My daughter said, "No, you will not! You have wanted to get your GED your whole life." My kids knew this secret and vowed never to share it. I was so ashamed of not graduating. Imagine being in a coffin and having dirt piled on top of you. That is exactly how I felt every day; carrying that weight was suffocating. So, I knew what had to be done. No way was I going to lie and put something not true, and indeed, God knew that about me. Oh, how I love Him.

The next day, I called a local place for info to get started. The lady on the other end asked me some questions and said it would take me 18–24 months. I said, "I don't have 18–24 months." You see, I only went for two weeks of 9th grade, so I was starting at ground zero and fully understood why they would say it would take that long, but I didn't have that long. So, I took a hiatus from coaching and everything else and went to work. I studied seven days a week, 7–8 hours a day. I finished the final test in eight weeks. Eight weeks!

I was so proud of myself. I completed what I started after more than four decades and no longer had to carry that shame. The day I found out I had passed the final test, I was so nervous to open the email that I made my husband do it. He looked at me, paused, and got choked up with tears in his eyes as he said, "YOU DID IT!" At that moment, I realized he had carried the weight with me all those years too and was so proud of me. What a beautiful moment that I will never forget.

Oh, the pressure that was mounting within me was so great when God uncapped my emotional well of being numb for forty years; it was as if my earth let out a shout and a torrent of tears that were finally uncapped. Every deep and dark thought and memory that I had buried in the pit of my soul came out. Every thought flowed over my mind just as it happened in real-time. I remember back when I wanted to die sitting in a tent on the beach when it was pouring rain. I remember the moments of tremendous hatred and bitterness. I remember feeling so alone at six years old on the porch as I cried my face off. I remember running away. I remember burying every single dream I had as though they never existed. This time, though, my emotional experience wasn't just an exercise in guilt and shame; this time was different. With each memory, Christ was there handing off my trauma for his gift and his sacrifice. He was assisting me in purging the dark and misconstrued, mischaracterized, confused, lost parts of me so I could receive from him the very thing that he desperately wanted me to have.

Finally, in my late forties, I was ready to receive the willowing ax that the Lord had in his hand, ready to chop down any tree that had exalted itself against the knowledge of God in my life. I was ready for Him to purge these deep, dark things in me. Here I am, with the Redeemer knocking on my door, ready to take upon Himself the pain and the trauma that I had experienced, but the only way I could proceed was to give Him my coping strategies as my atonement. He alone was My Sacrifice. I couldn't sugarcoat it anymore; no coping strategy that I've tried ever succeeded for me. No bearing the emotions, no avoiding my pain, no looking at the scars, no distraction, and no busyness could solve the void that I had inside except for Him.

He showed me a passage that was most fitting for my process. Matthew 19:24: "Again I tell you, it is easier for a camel to go through the eye of a needle than for someone who is rich to enter the kingdom of God." Many don't take the time to consider this verse's historical and geographical significance to actually understand it. Jesus is telling this man that to go through a very particular gate in Jerusalem, he must take off his baggage to fit through. This is what God was doing to me. For me to get through the gate that He had called me to, I needed to take off all of the extra baggage that I was accumulating and carrying with me.

Now that I was finally ready, the Lord showed himself faithful. God was good to me. He took me on a season of healing even after all these years and returned me back to my childhood, one moment at a time, one memory at a time, to bring me healing and closure.

Sometimes, He would show me visually where He was during those moments of trouble, moments of transition when my family relocated every six months, and moments of pain when I witnessed the abuse within my family. He showed me where He was. He brought me healing, and I did my very best to give Him my whole self for the first time. It wasn't easy, it's still not easy, but I'm trying to be willing because I know that's what He's asked of me.

Purging the Dark Places

Is it possible that when someone's born, they are given a purpose and destiny yet to be explored within their spirit? I believe this is the case, just as we see in the life of Tamar. Her participation is extremely important; nevertheless, she still had a purpose and a Destiny in her life. The magnitude of this purpose sometimes requires opposition to complete it. It may be hard for some to consider, but who did anything great in the Bible without opposition? Without personal turmoil or exterior forces of confusion and resistance? There are none to be mentioned, including Jesus.

Why does this give us such significance today? Regardless of the magnitude of our purpose, we will all encounter opposition, labels, confusion, lack of identity, displacement, and accusations that misplace us for decades on end. It's almost promised because it's so frequent. Nevertheless, our willingness to purge the Dark Places that we find Within ourselves is a prerequisite for our righteousness in him. Yes, we receive Him as our Eternal savior, but what about our hearts and our minds today? Yes, we are sealed unto the day of redemption. But what about our Legacy and purpose today?

Our response is truly the only thing that matters. Some would go and measure their wounds and tribulation against others and say they had it worse; therefore, they're justified in their scars, and they're justified in their immobility. Some may say they were mistreated so severely they have just cause to not move in their purpose. Some may say they were so misunderstood they have reason to continue in their plight. It is not the magnitude of what is committed against us but rather our ability to respond that keeps us righteous. If we were to measure what came against Christ, we would have the longest list ever created. He endured every temptation known to man. This is not a list worth considering, but rather, how did he respond to what was leveled against him?

You alone have permission to move forward and purge the places of darkness that remain Within. This was not possible before because you didn't have a helper. Now you do. Christ wants to exchange a measure for a measure with you. He wants to take that sorrow, pain, and hurt and give you mercy, grace, and peace in its place. He wants to mend every broken place in your heart, mind, and body so that you can fulfill your destiny. Even if it's taken you years to come to this place, just as it took me over forty years, allow him to purge the dark places of your heart so you can move on to what he's called you to do.

Woman, where are you? Why are you hiding? Who told you to be afraid?

Come near me. Lie on my chest just as John the Beloved did. Do you hear my heartbeat? Can you feel every time I breathe? I am here with you. I've been here the whole time. I knew you before I fashioned you in your mother's womb. I know everything there is to know about you. I know about your insecurities, failures, and the areas where you feel you've fallen short. I still call you mine.

No idea or person can ever take that away from me. You are mine. You're worth to me exceeds the stars in the heavens. I love you so much that I sent my son to come and redeem you unto me. You will never fully understand the love that I have for you. Ask me. Ask me where I was when you were let down. Ask me where I was when you felt like the world failed you or I failed you. I will show you every moment where I was and how I was supporting you, comforting you, helping you.

There's nothing under the sun that my son Jesus hasn't overcome and experienced for himself. He is the most relatable person who has ever walked the Earth. In Him alone, you will see the answer to every question your heart raises. Don't be afraid. I can carry your burden. Allow me to share in your pain. Let me into your heart because I can help. You are my beloved. It's time to trade your trauma for my love. Give me your guilt and shame; I will clothe you with purity and righteousness. Give me your pain, and I will give you healing. Give me a free-will offering, and I will give you salvation. I am the Lord your God, and nothing will separate me from loving you.

God

Coming Out of the Cave

Everyone has seen the beautiful picture of the footprints in the sand. It's a picture that describes an experience that we have with God. We are walking side by side With God, but then there's only one set of footprints left. Many wonder if God left them alone but then find out He was actually carrying them. Sometimes, we see one set of footprints and think they are our own, but then we realize we are being carried. That is the definition of healing.

Elijah, in the Old Testament, was on the run after he found out someone wanted him dead. He was afraid, fearing for his life; he just wanted to die. He was contemplating within himself if he should live anymore. The fear and the pain were so deep even someone so great as Elijah was broken and vulnerable. I'm sure Elijah asked himself, How could this happen to me? What did I do wrong? Regardless of the questions and confusion, God was there to help.

Then Elijah walked for a whole day into the desert. He sat down under a bush and asked to die. "I have had enough, Lord," he prayed. "Let me die. I am no better than my ancestors." (1 Kings 19:3–4)

Elijah then lay down to take a nap. Sometimes, when we're so broken, the only option is to lie down, curl up in a little ball just as we were when we were a baby, and take a nap. This is the position of submission. Elijah was finally ready to let God lead him. This is the introduction to purging and the beginning of healing.

Why would someone so strong and powerful be shaken by someone so weak? Elijah had some healing to do. He had to rid himself of those fissures and tethers that made him so vulnerable that he would forget who he was. The Apostle Paul says that we should die daily to ourselves in order to start the adoption of working out our salvation. This was Elijah's process of dying to himself. Clearly, his heart was filled with fear, and he was motivated by things other than what God had for him. A purging of himself was required.

Suddenly, an angel came to him and touched him. "Get up and eat," the angel said. Elijah saw near his head a loaf baked over coals and a jar of water, so he ate and drank. Then he went back to sleep. Later, the Lord's angel came to him a second time. The angel touched him and said, "Get up and eat. If you don't, the Journey will be too hard for you." So Elijah got up and ate and drank. The food made him strong enough to walk to Mount Sinai, the Mountain of God, for forty days and nights. There, Elijah went into a cave and stayed all night. (1 Kings 19:5–8)

Elijah was strengthened by God's food in between a few naps. He then felt strong enough to go on a perfected Journey to rid himself of the devil. See, a fly's life expectancy is forty days, and the Lord of the Flies (the devil) Wants to take residency in our thoughts, emotions, and lives. In the case of Elijah and so many others in the Bible, including Jesus, they were to go on a forty-day and forty-night Journey to rid themselves of anything that was not from God.

Yes, God was leading Elijah through the forty days and forty nights just as the Father God led Jesus through the forty days and forty nights. This picture of purging is visualized in the story of Shadrach, Meshach, and Abednego. They were sentenced to burn up in a fire. Nebuchadnezzar ordered the fire to be seven times hotter than normal, and the three men were thrown in with everything they had on Into the Fire. Then, Nebuchadnezzar stood up and said, "Did we not throw three men into the fire?" He was amazed.

He answered and said, "Lo, I see four men loose, walking in the midst of the fire, and they have no hurt; and the form of the fourth is like the Son of God." (Daniel 3:25)

When we're going through difficult times and we're feeling

persecuted and under duress, when our accusers have placed us in the fire, if we open our eyes, we will realize that the Son of God is standing next to us in the midst of the fire. Of course, it's seven times hotter to make sure our impurities are burned up and only Christ remains.

The forty-day and forty-night journey is to bring us to the end of ourselves. It's to bring us to the end of our human strength. This realization and experience is also a gift from God. You may ask, how could this be a gift from God? Simply put, God can't lead you when you're leading yourself. He's a jealous God who wants to be first in your heart if your heart is filled with many lovers, idols, sin, and fear. How could He lead you? If you are a divided mind and you serve two masters, which way should you go? Confusion abounds for those who get lost in the wilderness.

Not everybody who left Egypt made it into the Promised Land. There are many who decided within themselves that they had a better way than God's way for their lives. The result for them was that they would die in the wilderness. They never made it to the promised land. Sometimes, our heart is filled with so many idols, sin, and fear that we don't allow God in to lead. This is why we all go through the forty-day and forty-night Journey. It's so that we can get to the end of ourselves and He can start to lead.

After a season of running away, we all need immense healing. Of course, the healing is not all at once. It does take some time and intentionality. Depending on the healing Journey that we find ourselves in, some longer than others, we are not yet ready to embrace the fullness of God, so we are led into the cave, just as God led Elijah into the cave. The cave embodies a hiddenness and external protection that we seek when we're in a season of feeling vulnerable. God comes along not only to bandage our wounds but to heal them from the inside out. The Healer starts with the heart before anything else. Oftentimes, He works on our hearts so much and for so long that it offends our minds. Why am I here? What am I doing? Why is this taking so long? He quiets our minds so He can demonstrate surgical precision to extract every piece of scar tissue and every cancerous thing that will destroy us.

When we are at the end of ourselves and don't have anything left, we feel naked and alone because we are. We have more questions than answers because nothing seems to work, because now we have nothing. However, this is the start of our new season. We needed to come to this place for us to walk in our new life. Finally, God can begin His new work when we are done leading ourselves.

Jesus proclaims you must be born again to enter the kingdom of heaven. Everyone around him was so confused by this statement. "Shall we reenter our mother's womb?" they say. No, those born of the Flesh are born of the Flesh, and those born of the spirit are born of the spirit. Today is the first day that you are called out of the cave. The cave has always been a symbolic womb that you were called to go into so that you could be born out of it! God the Father speaks to Elijah in the most quintessential way and says, "Elijah! Why are you here?"

Doesn't God have a sense of humor? He's been with Elijah this entire time, actually leading him and sustaining him, and then He asks Elijah, what are you doing in the cave? It's because Elijah was never meant to stay in the cave and should not identify with it. Do you remember the Father God asking Adam and Eve the same question? What are you doing? Where are you? God's not surprised; He's not asking the question for information. He's reminding us that we should not associate our identity with the cave.

The Lord said to Elijah, *"Go, stand in front of me on the mountain, and I will pass by you." Then, a very strong wind blew until it caused the mountains to fall apart and large rocks to break in front of the Lord. But the Lord was not in the wind. After the wind, there was an earthquake, but the Lord was not in the earthquake. After the earthquake, there was a fire, but the Lord was not in the fire. After the fire, there was a quiet, gentle sound. When Elijah heard it, he covered his face with his coat and stood at the cave entrance.* (1 Kings 19:11–13)

God removed the mountains in the strongholds in Elijah's life. He pushed the big boulders out of the way. He brought great shaking with the wind and the earthquakes to move the foundations. Once the foundations were moved, God set everything on fire just as He did with Moses. Now, at the place of perfection and purity, a quiet and gentle sound embraced Elijah. God then asked him a second time, "Elijah, why are you here?" Elijah said, "There's no one else;

I'm all alone," and God said, "No, there are many others, and I'll take you to them." This is when Elijah gets his new assignment, and he leaves the cave a different person. Now, he was perfected in his faith, and the devil had nothing in him. Every Mountain had been moved, every foundation was shaken, everything that was weak without roots was blown away, everything that was dead was burned up, and now Elijah could finally enter his new season. Elijah stood at the cave entrance and entered a born-again state. He was accepting of the Salvation of the Lord!

Sometimes, we go into the cave in order to come out of it. It's a required step for those who want to get rid of everything they know to adopt Christ. The soul is ready to be awakened when we give it the right set of conditions. When we remove all of the artificial support that we've given ourselves, when we cease the day of coping mechanisms and Band-Aids and realize that we wholeheartedly need to embrace Christ, we are saved and can come out of the cave.

When God Brought Me Out of the Cave

My desire for this new season of My Life brought me out of my cave. Perhaps I was in a self-induced cave for forty years, just like the Israelites. The reasons for my induced hiddenness were part of my transformation. Regardless of the effects that others had upon me, I was going through a transformation. With Christ's help, I decided I would allow him to help me get rid of those things that bound me and kept me hidden. I desperately wanted to work on what kept me from leaving this cave of my own making. See, I realized we're all called to go on the Journey that brings us to the end of ourselves. I accepted this ownership and New Birth the day I came out of the cave. And fully understood that glory carriers do not hide in caves.

I worked hard for forty years, burying every deep and negative emotion, intrusive thought, and bad experience that violated the purity of who I was. This was my practice, and I learned very well from those around me how to deal with such things. I had no idea the level of deep, hidden trauma that I carried with me over the decades. It was only revealed to me slowly and surgically as God presented me with my own Heart considerations and traumas while He simultaneously gave me the answer for each one. Occasionally, I felt like my heart was ripped out of my chest. It was behind so much scar tissue that anything was painful. Some days, He was working on my quiet anger; others, He was working on my shame. This went on for years. As I saw Him, a layer of my heart was made new.

Sometimes, He would show me my past and allow me to revisit the origins of such trauma to show me His Redemptive perspective. This brought me so much healing because I could finally see my life through the eyes of redemption and freedom. It took many years for me to unpack four decades of being numb. Still, to this day, my heart is tender in some areas. Perhaps it will always be as I continue to meet with Him about it. In my weakness, He is made strong and perfected in my faith. I realized He just wanted my yes; He didn't want my perfection.

I'm no longer standing in the fire alone, but I'm standing in the fire with the one perfected in the flame. Once I arrived at the end of myself, I had to actually give God all of me. I had to hand over those negative thoughts, feelings, doubts, beliefs, and any reservations in my heart. Only then could I take ownership and responsibility for my life deeply and meaningfully. Before, I was just existing, and now I was partnering with God to bring about my purpose and calling. Of course, the natural thing to do was to get my house in order, so I went back, took care of my education, and ensured that simple things would no longer hold me back.

I was motivated to come out of this season of hiding. I know on the outside, getting my GED didn't mean anything, but to me, it did, so I had to complete it. Everyone in my family had graduated except for me. Some could not understand why I wanted it, considering I was already a successful businesswoman, wife, mother, and grandmother, and I carried the title of becoming the first millionaire in my family. They would say, "You're the poster image of being 'self made.'" I fully understood what they were saying and knew it came as a compliment. However I knew the shame of not having graduated; they did not. It was for me, not anyone else. That Christmas, I opened my present from my kids, and to my surprise, they had gotten me a Class of 2022 ring.

As I continue to assess my season of hiddenness, I realize God allowed me to stay hidden because I wasn't ready. I still carried fissures and broken places in my heart. If I stepped out of the cave too early, I would be a lamb before a slaughter. The world would have eaten me up just as it did in the past. Instead, I wait until my faith is perfected in Him, and He positions Himself to take the payment for my sin and my transgressions. He sends Himself out as a lamb before a slaughter to the world's wolves. He conquers the Brunt of accusation, pain, drama, lies, slander, and labels. This is when He turns back to me in the cave and says:

"My beloved, follow me. You are my delight and my joy. The time is up for you to remain hidden. Though your heart may be tender, it's mine. I've removed everything that doesn't belong there. I want you to start thinking like me. I've put too much of my heart and my spirit into you for you to be trapped and bound any longer. Follow me into your new season. You are not alone, and you never were. I've been here the whole time, and there are many others who are just like you. Tell me again why you are here. The time is now! Follow me as we leave this place, not to forget it but to move on! You have a purpose and a calling that goes beyond your comprehension. I have been dreaming about the days that you walk into. You are my delight, and I will be with you."

Rebekah

Rebekah is a perfect example of someone who leaves the cave. In

Genesis 24 is a story of a woman who said yes when she had no idea what the future held for her. Her story drips with the sweet fragrance of the rose of Sharon. In verse 58, we find her family asking her, "Will you go be with this man Isaac, whom you've never seen?" Rebekah says something so fearless and open; she says, "I will go." So, her family blesses her and says, "Go and be the mother of millions and possess the gate." She arises and rides upon the camels through the hot desert with Isaacs's servant leading the way. I'm sure she looked many times at the bracelets upon her hands placed there by the servant from orders of Isaac.

What a beautiful picture of what happens next. Isaac is in the desert and deep in thought when he sees movement. Maybe for a minute, he thinks his mind is playing tricks on him. No, it's the camels coming with his soon-to-be bride Rebekah. Rebekah sees Isaac and asks the servant, "Who is this man walking in the desert to meet us?" The servant says, "It is my master Isaac," so she takes her veil and covers herself. The Bible says he took Rebekah as his wife and loved her.

The very picture of Christ, our Redeemer, is fully displayed in this story. He adorns us with his gifts and equips us for life's Journey when we say yes to the unknown. Yes to climbing the camel and following wherever he leads. We may not know the address of where we're going, but we trust in him to take us there. If we find ourselves on the wrong road, he'll be there as well. His love is unfailing, unending, and everlasting.

Power Is in Our Yes

The question of the century is: how much power has God placed in our decision-making process? Is not the Father the most fantastic Galactic gentleman that He would wait patiently with long-suffering for our yes? So many people look at their indifference and unchangeable realities and question God. Why would you put me here? Why have I been here so long? Little did they know the Journey they were on was the one that saved them not only for today but also for their soul for eternity. Why didn't God intervene sooner? Shall He make void your free will and choice for the greater good? No! Relationships are birthed out of choice, not control. We are without excuse in our assessment of God's goodness. He does not break the rules. He does not lie; therefore, we can trust Him and realize He was waiting on us the whole time. What are we waiting for?

Life of Redemption

What is the difference between our state walking into the cave and our state walking out of it? On the outside, we still look at ourselves in the mirror and see the same wrinkles, imperfections, and things we dislike. Our hair is the same color, and our nose is not quite the right size. We look the same as we once did. What's the difference? We did so on our own strength when we walked into the cave. When we walk out of the cave, we do so in the strength of God. The Spirit of God strengthens us from within, and we can profess, "I no longer live, but it is Christ who lives in me." Our realization of this transformation will be ever unfolding. We will realize the partnership in the unveiling daily for the rest of our lives. Suddenly, everything about you changed, but you have not yet realized it. Your birthright changed, but you have not yet seen your lineage to know who your Father is. It will take some time for you to understand your new position in life.

Confusion abounds in a wandering life, and the potential for confusion abounds Evermore when you are instilled with such promise as to be in Christ. What's the point of Salvation today if you were to find no value in it? Is it simply a proposition for tomorrow when your eyes are closed and you're sleeping? Absolutely not. Surely, salvation is defined as the seal unto the Lord for a life of everlastingness in him. Is there an effect on my life today with this Everlasting seal? The devil proposes confusion amid denominations on this subject. He would have you saved and useless in your life today. Heaven is sure on this matter, though. That is why we received Christ in the flesh and recognize his Redemptive work on the Earth as a type and a shadow. You, too, are to be redeemed. Your life and your story are beautiful to me.

Many ask, How can I possibly bring a benefit to myself or to God? You are no longer yourself. You are His. Did you forget your transaction with Jesus? He purchased your sin, pain, suffering, insecurities, and anger. It belongs to Him now. If you should dabble in it again, you are breaking the contract between you and God. Did not those things die with your former self in the cave? Shall you resurrect your sin and entertain it further? No. If you are born again and you live in Christ Jesus, then you must die daily to your former self and put on the mind of Christ, for you are not your own.

Once you are found trustworthy in carrying His name, He'll give you access to His heart and reveal things about yourself and the world around you that you have not even begun to imagine. Trust takes time and faithfulness. Those who are proven to be faithful are rewarded with an abundant life. This new life that God calls us to is measured by repentance. Our souls can be saved, but our minds can remain unchanged. When we see ourselves, we are a reflection of our mind and our heart. This is why we are invited to allow the word of God to discern the thoughts and the intents of our hearts. Repentance invites us to change one thought at a time from what we used to think and replace it with how He thinks. One thought for one thought. This is only possible because of redemption.

When we give our lives to God, we give our whole lives to God. Our past is no longer our own, but it is bought with the precious blood of Jesus Christ. In Leviticus, it clearly says that life is in the blood. That's why Jesus shed his blood for us. Therefore, anytime we revisit our past, we do so through the Redemptive blood of Jesus Christ. He is the only lens through which we are able to see our past. If we visit our past without the lens of Jesus being our savior and Redeemer, who purchased everything from us so that we could have an abundant life in him, then we are violating the terms of our agreement. Jesus says he is the door; no one should come in or go out any other way. If they choose to return any other way, they are thieves and robbers. Most assuredly, I tell you this is good news. No digging up our former selves! He revisits our past and considers us forgiven.

What Does He Say About Us?

Infancy creates a natural dependency on health and sustainability. When you're born again, you become absolutely dependent upon God. He becomes a lifeline, a voice of reason, a breath of fresh air to someone who doesn't know their way yet. Infants also have a vulnerability to them that is unmatched at any other point in their life. The sustenance they need just to get through the day is dependent upon their caregiver. At this stage, it's natural to doubt our past and our thought processes less; they lead us astray again. When we are commanded to let go of the former things and not stare at the pictures on the wall of where we used to live and who we used to be, we question our ability to make good decisions. We question our ability to find the truth. That is why we need God to guide us. The way that He chooses to guide us is with His voice.

Biblically speaking, God gives His voice to His children, and His children know His voice. How is this possible? It's possible because you're now in Christ Jesus, who has given you his Spirit. That's how His voice can lead you. Practically speaking, we have the word of God as a written narration and invitation into the voice of God. Jesus embodied the word and wrapped the word up into himself, and so everything in the Bible points back to Jesus. Secondarily, he gave us his Spirit to remember all he spoke. So, we have the written and spoken word of God speak to us about God's perfectly good and acceptable will for our lives. Not just to have a principled life but to have a presence-driven life.

Now that you've rid your mind of the former things, it's time to ask the Deep, meaningful questions that will change your life. What does God say about you? Inquiring into the mind of God will not only unlock your identity because He made you, but it will also unlock your potential. It is our lifelong pursuit to inquire upon the will of God for our lives. The first thing we shall do once we exit the cave is to remind ourselves of who He is and what He's done and allow Him to remind us of His unwavering faithfulness toward us. The Holy Spirit will never resist the opportunity to shower us with love and affection from God. Remember, your mind can't serve two masters, so if you are ready, allow God to fill you, but don't return to the critic and the heretic that creeps in between your ears and feeds you sour milk. The evil voices will leaven and grow and leave you malnourished and confused. So, do away with the former things and allow God's voice to speak to you about the tiny things and about the big things in your life.

Jesus Embodied Love

In the scriptures, we read stories of Hero's Journeys. Some stories start off with a villain, while others start off with the victor. This is a common frame of understanding that people see. However, the Bible is a relational book written to someone in love. It's deep and complex, yes. It's relationally demanding and leaves curiosity and questions outstanding. This is the intention of every good love story. To begin to understand this love, you have to trust.

Something that's only possible if you walk in with blind love and acceptance. This is what the Bible calls faith.

This love story is conveyed in many ways in the minute details of the Life of Christ, those who came before him, and those who came after him. We can see that the names of God and the actions of Christ embody a Heavenly love that the Earth has never seen. So, we happily embrace the Compassion of Christ for ourselves as we reconstruct our identity. There are Bountiful love stories within the bigger love story that speak to us about the nature of God and how He sees us. We are invited to partake of His word day and night until we are changed. Imagine a groom pursuing his bride with love and affection. What would hold him back if Heaven was behind him and supporting him in showering her with praises? What shall he say to woo her at the beginning of their relationship? Allow these words to speak over you.

Woman, I'm so proud of you. You are cherished and loved beyond comprehension. My thoughts about you are endless. Oh, my love. Let me remind you: I define beauty, and I made you. You are my tender shoot. No matter your mood, you're still my lily of the valley. Come to me and rest. Where can you go without my heart? Lean into me and find yourself, not out there with the clowns and imitators. I know you better than anyone else. I record your moments in my heart and anticipate our future together. Your future will be endless and bountiful now that you're in me. Come and see the way that I see things. Come up here, my beloved.

I stretch my hands over you as your grace and shade. You can find rest in Me. When your days grow weary and your decisions are blurry, come to me and I will give you rest. Do I not meticulously tend to the birds of the air to make sure they have enough food? Surely, I will have enough for you when you ask of me. I desire to take you to places that you cannot even imagine. Will you trust me and come with me? I stretched the heavens from the East to the West to come and be with you. I sent you my Son as your Redeemer. You can partake in his thoughts and heart at any point you choose. If I am with you, who could be against you? If you are in my Son, who can be against you? I know sometimes you may be confused by circumstance, but my love should never be questioned. I, along with Heaven, stand to support, heal, and love you so that you can become the greatest version of yourself. I am your greatest advocate. I am the Lord your God.

God

Redemptive Lens of Christ

If we should return and observe our former selves, then we should do so with the Redemptive lens of Christ. We shall see him as Our Redeemer; through Him, we see our past. We see His payment for the person we once were, and we see His perspective about our situation and no longer our own perspective. This changes everything. This gives me access to the most defining moments in my past, but now I get to see it through His Redemptive eyes. This changed everything for me because any moment I felt let down in my past, He could show me a redemption process, a vision, and comfort to keep pursuing my life, purpose, and calling.

We are called to the ministry of reconciliation first to ourselves and then to everyone around us. The invitation for us is to embrace the moment we're saved. We start to reconcile ourselves to the Lord, revisit every relationship we have, and either reconcile our past or present relationships with God. Simply put, I am a changed person, and now I need to revisit every relationship I've ever had with the lens of God through Redemption. This starts with me first. I need to accept every part of me under the work of Christ to begin my new identity. Forgiveness is the beginning of our new life. We must forgive ourselves using the power of forgiveness that God gives us.

Establishing our identity based on the word of God and the will of God is essential. Up until the point when I embraced him, I established my identity based on my accomplishments, failures, and the things that had happened to me in the past. An example would be if I were a sponge, picking up whatever I encountered and adopting it as my identity. This is what most people do. They think their identity is a composite of all the thoughts and dreams they have, and good and bad experiences. This is not the case for those who are children of God. Their identity comes from God. Not only are we made in God's image, but we are also made to think, live, and behave as God intended.

The identity of God is clearly seen in the life of Jesus. We see the heart of the Father and the fulfillment of Christ in ourselves based on his association with the Father. It's upside down from what we have known. God knows that we will struggle with this, so He gives us His mind to think about this instead of Our Own. It's a spiritual principle of adopting the mind of Christ. It is not just symbolic; the Holy Spirit helps us with this by bringing to remembrance all things Christ said. The vastness of the word of God testifies about Jesus to us.

When the Father looks Upon Jesus, does He see someone broken and frail? No, He does not. He sees His beloved Son, who is King, seated at the Father's right hand. He sees no weakness, no lack of love, only never-ending Mercy. He sees perfection. The best part about this relationship is that we are in Christ Jesus. We alone have a lot of work to do to start accepting this new reality. When God sees us, He sees the redemptive life of Jesus. We are covered and cleansed in Him and by Him. We should start acting like it instead of acting like our former selves.

Once we're good and ready to return to the world, let's use our testimony for good. Right after I was saved, I was on fire for God. Every week, I would go up in front of the church and tell my story, hoping it might help someone else just as it helped me. Sure enough, this is a biblical principle discussed in Revelation 19:10: the testimony of Jesus is the Spirit of Prophecy. My interpretation of this verse is that if I'm in Christ and share my story, it activates something in Heaven or on Earth to partner with what God wants to do in people's lives. I prophesy in their life when I share my story.

I became familiar with a story a few years ago that I have never forgotten. A man had visited Israel and this is what he said he learned. One time, while visiting Israel, he went to a museum and saw a small brass buck in the corner with several wooden poles intricately marked with symbols from the bottom to the top. He asked a curator what they were, and with broken English, he said, "Rods of testimony." He signaled for another member of the staff to come who could explain. What they shared between them brought a significant revelation of scripture into my own life.

They shared that as a child came to the "age of understanding, they would be given a clean shaft of wood (about a meter long) and a knife." As they had significant encounters with God, they would carve a symbol or sign into the wood from the bottom to the top. This man was faced with the spiritual diary of some folk long dead—each symbol representing something significant in their lives. I kept them talking far longer than they wanted and left feeling I needed to have a really good look at any scripture that could back this talk up.

What unfolded then was months of investigation. Looking at Psalm 23—"Thy Rod and Staff comfort me." In Hebrews 11:21, Jacob leaned on the top of his staff. In Numbers 17, Moses asked for each of the leaders of the tribes to bring an unmarked staff into the tent of meeting; the successor of Israel's staff would buy Almonds— Aaron's staff was also placed into the Ark of the Covenant.

One account of the 84 references in scripture I found jumped out at me. In Exodus 14:16, Moses was told by God to "lift up your Rod and stretch out your hand..." I had to ask why. In that passage, Moses—the reluctant deliverer—boldly proclaimed to stand still and see the Salvation of the Lord. The Jews had a sea in front of them, a desert on one side, mountains on the other, and the Egyptians behind them.

In the next verse, after such a proclamation, God asks Moses, "Why are you crying." The leader of Israel was bold but internally was full of fear and doubt. The advice God gave Moses that day was to place the testimony of God's goodness between him and the problem—no doubt the rod of testimony obscured the circumstance and built faith. In our lives, we need to make an appointment with God and review all the times in our lives He has spoken to us, blessed us, and answered our prayers. Even when He's been silent, or the answer was not what we wanted, it still may have proved to be the best answer for us over time.

I always said, Lord, my testimony is yours if you can use my story for your glory. This is what I would do all the time. I would raise my hand at church every week and thank God for saving me, and I wanted to teach and serve as much as I could because I was just so excited to give back. One of my first serving places was with the little kids and the babies. I had a captive audience. They could only crawl away. The Bible says we overcome and are Overcomers by the word of Our Testimony. For three years, I had perfect attendance at the first church I landed at. That little country gospel Baptist Church, that is where I learned to fall in love with God's word. Clifton Powers was the Pastor. He took the time to disciple me. He would say, Mika, you have to know the word of God for yourself. Do not depend on someone to feed you the word. You have to eat it daily. I took what he said and applied every word. I stayed in my Bible day and night for years. I was afraid not to. The more I read, the more I fell in love with Christ.

Then I moved to a Full Gospel Church and this is where I learned that God indeed speaks to us through dreams and visions. And that the gifts of the spirit are for all who would receive them. This is also where I was called to preach the gospel. I was sitting in the front pew that Sunday night. When God spoke and said, "Mika, I have called you to preach to the nations," I did not tell anyone except my husband when I got home. Of course, I'm the first generation woman preacher in our bloodline.

I felt the invitation to share even though I knew I wasn't perfect because I felt like it was the least I could do for God after everything He'd done for me. Also, I was just so excited to share. I was radical. I was like a kid in a candy store. Every day I went to church, I realized something amazing about what God had given me, and I was so thankful for what He brought me. I remember the day when I found out that God gave us gifts and that we could partner with Him and serve Him in different ways. Everything was like a Christmas unboxing party.

Fast forward to today. That's the purpose of this book. I want my story to go as far as God will take it so that He may be glorified and people might be redeemed. I want this for you as well. Your story is yours to tell, and God can be glorified in it. Also, it can be the tool that unlocks your next season because God Will Not Waste His investment in you. When you adopt Christ's mind and start thinking like him, you might as well behave like him, and everything around you will begin to change. Because you were in him, I can gladly say your life is redeemed, and your future looks bright.

Women Full of Wonder

A beautiful thing happens on the road from the cave. Now that you've finally submitted your life to God, He looks at you and says, "What do you want to do?" If you're perplexed by this question and have no idea how to respond, you have yet to realize your new position. You are a woman full of wonder. There's this thing called Progressive truth in the Bible. At one point, the people of Israel were passing through the desert of Egypt. They eventually made it to their Promised Land. Looking at the Bible, we can easily see this progression: they're no longer in Egypt, and now they're in the Promised Land. The same concept applies to spiritual truth.

John the Baptist's job was to usher in the coming King. However, he embodied a time and place to be fulfilled and done away with for Jesus to come. John famously said, "I'm not worthy to tie your sandals." In John 3:30, he says he must increase, but I must decrease. This was absolutely true for John the Baptist. He was not supposed to have a superior ministry to Jesus. He should fulfill his purpose and allow Jesus to usher in His Heavenly purpose. Then, he looks unto the disciples and issues his Spirit to them. Jesus says in Luke 24, "I send my Father's promise to you, that you may be endued with power from on high." In Hebrew, the word "power" here is "dunamis," which means force. And when we are in Christ, we are a force to be reckoned with.

Perhaps, when you were in the cave, it was appropriate for you to embody the words of John the Baptist. At that time in your life, you did need to decrease so that he could increase. However, if you reject yourself now that you are in him, you are rejecting the work of the cross. If you deny yourself the ability he has given you, you reject the reward of Jesus. If you pray that you may decrease so that he may increase, you don't realize you're in him and disregard the progressive truth. Why would God invest more of Himself and you if you reject His investments and say they're worthless?

Repentance is necessary to sustain the progressive truth that is upon us. You are not allowed to say that you are worthless anymore. You can't even think it, lest you go against the investment He made in you. You can't say you're not beautiful anymore, lest you deny the Masterpiece He made. You can no longer deny the love that's been given to you. Christ gives perfect love; how could you reject it? You're a different person now. You are a woman of wonder who embodies the word of God.

My Yes

There comes a time in our faith journey when our yes becomes louder than our no. If I felt like God was telling me to do something, my yes was so loud that nothing else came between us. It was no longer what I wanted; I would steer my decisions based on what He wanted. My Yes came from a cultivated time of being in His word, praying, fasting and listening to the teachings of others. I could see answered prayer in my life. This didn't mean that every one of my situations or circumstances changed for the better. I still lived my life amid this good and evil world. However, now I had Him, when before I didn't. So, anytime He asked me to do something, or I felt like He was leading me to do something, I would say yes. I remember one time I was walking into a store and this couple had walked past me. God said, "Go tell them my grace is sufficient." I said, "God, I can't do that, all the while knowing I was going to obey." As I told the couple, tears streamed down their faces. They said they had been praying for a specific word about the situation they were in. Well, that word was exactly the word I gave them. God uses me all the time now in that way, and I never get over the awe of Him and His loving kindness toward His people. Mankind is His people. And He is concerned about all matters we face in life.

I started cleaning houses when I was just a young girl, not

knowing anything about business. The number of houses I cleaned over time grew, but it reached a critical point in 2003. I remember a very specific moment when I was in my car talking to God about my struggling business. I turned on my car radio, and TD Jakes popped on, and the voice coming out of the speakers sounded like thunder, just as God would reveal Himself during specific occasions in the Bible. All I remember Him saying was when people get tired of being broke, they do something about it. This sparked an unquenchable fire in me. I decided to make God my business partner and told Him to teach me how to run a good business. I opened myself up to hear what God had to say about my business and how He could help me. In return, even though He's a generous God and doesn't need anything, I pledged to always share Him with anyone I encounter because He's that good. So, I've been on a journey ever since. Of course, I've continued to make mistakes and failed many times, but I've always gotten back up and partnered with Him. I always wanted God to be more than willing to partner with me in any endeavor I might pursue. Therefore, that meant I didn't make a single move or make a decision without consulting my business partner.

Over the years, the growth has been unbelievable. From our humble days of having one or seven different houses, to over 300 houses that we now provide services for. I have an office and employees. I'm beyond blessed to partner with God in this endeavor, and my family is blessed because of my partnership. I made it a point to always say yes to Him in business and life. My Yes didn't remove any obstacles; it simply aligned me to be on the right page with God amid my obstacles. Of course, He's blessed me tremendously, but I would partner with God even if I didn't have what I do now because He is the ultimate reward over any material thing.

Every time I say yes to Him, it's as if a piece of my heart is properly aligned with His. Every time I digest one small piece of His word, it's as if my mind has changed a little. Slowly and surely, my mind and heart accept the identity they've always wanted in God. I know I was made in His image, but the excitement that transpires in our hearts and Minds when we are properly aligned with our maker is unimaginable. The Bible says that all of Heaven celebrates when someone gets saved. I wonder what happens in Heaven when someone continuously partners with God and works out their Salvation daily.

Are we called to embody love and manifest it on Earth? I believe we are because we are women of wonder. We are made in God's likeness with His divine nature flowing through our veins. We are unstoppable. When properly aligned with Him, we can ask of the Father, seek His heart, and knock on every opportunity in front of us because we are His. Who can say no to someone who's in Christ Jesus? Opportunity in Him is just the beginning. Not selfishly, but it's to partake in the reward of Christ. If we are truly the joy set before Him, then let us embrace the joy in life and become the very thing that He imagined us to become.

Nothing is holding us back now. We are women full of wonder

who have no limitations, according to God. Who can come to God and say this is not available, and that is not available? If God gave you a vision, then how could He not provide for the vision? Is not Heaven in full support of Jesus? It doesn't matter what anyone else says. If we are in Christ, then Heaven is fully supporting us. We are women full of wonder. Women of nobility, desire, Beauty, mystery, creation, and intellect, and we multiply everything we touch.

The beauty of life now is to find the sweet spot of contentment in Christ while pursuing his destiny and dreams for us. Are we not supposed to enjoy our partnership with God? Some would have you fear the world around you, but if you fear God, you will find your contentment and peace. If you are in Christ, you are placed in the person of peace. What should move you amid the storm? Nothing. You are a woman full of wonder made for this time. Have you not considered the unimaginable calculations it took to get you to be here right now. For some reason, you thought you had something to do with it. He sits in Heaven and laughs. You are predestined in His heart for such a time as this.

As I have forgiven my father for all of his decisions during my childhood, my heart has such a love for him. I know if he could change the past, he would in a second. When I got saved, he gave me my first Bible. It's the only Bible I've had in twenty-seven years. I've had it rebound twice from the worn pages. It travels with me no matter where I go. On the inside, it says, "Mika, I'm so proud of you. Love, Dad."

Hello, Woman Who Lacks Nothing

It is time that you embrace the pursuit before you. Consider the field and buy it! Did you know there were others before you who rejected the purpose and call in their life? Today, you have the opportunity to take Heaven into your hands. In the Gospels, it says the Kingdom of Heaven is at hand. The most applicable application of that verse is that the Kingdom of Heaven is like a throttle that you would thrust forth or pull back. You can pull Heaven into your day, life, and family because you're in Him. What are you waiting for, woman who lacks nothing? If you see the field, why don't you buy it? Ownership is your birthright. What are you pursuing?

Did you not know that complete freedom is available to you? Where you can experience love to its fullest extent and deploy boundaries for those who don't want to respect and honor the love that you have. You're not limited anymore by the things that you once were. It's okay if your emotions perk up sometimes about the past. Allow them to speak to you; you can remind them of how things are different now. We are perfected in him, yet we are not perfect. We exchange thoughts for thoughts and emotions for emotions with Christ. We continue to create within ourselves because we are made like him in his image. This means we need to continually partner with him to walk in complete freedom. This is not a one-and-done experience. We are invited to work out our Salvation daily and take every thought captive.

Yes, God wants to partner with us to manage every thought so it might not exalt itself against the knowledge of God. Freedom is much easier to embrace when you're surrounded by it. That is why we are placed in Him. When we are wrapped in purity and endued with power from on high, we start to embrace it as our own. The freedom that we hear about now becomes the freedom that we know. The freedom that we know is the freedom that we begin to live, and our behaviors are last to follow in line.

Indecision is just a fancy word for being double-minded. Those who are in Christ set about their work vigorously and are strengthened by their tasks. Is he not made strong in our weakness? Who should we be waiting for? You are a woman full of wonder who lacks nothing of value. Has he not spread the heavens open to reveal himself to you? Why should we be indecisive about the small and minute things? We shall have no fear for tomorrow because tomorrow worries for itself.

Are you lost, looking for a place to go? Are you stuck wondering what God has for you? Return back to the last place where He talked to you, and that's where He will meet you. He will rekindle those Desires in you now that you're properly aligned. It's time to start seeing yourself as His daughter seated in Christ Jesus, resting in His works. You are no longer your own. Is He not responsible for your value Watch? What you must say about yourself because you are talking about Him now. He may see things in you that you have not even imagined. You should trust Him because He's actually never failed you.

You know that feeling you get when you're in love, and your brain is clouded because the love is so overwhelming? That's where He wants to take you because sometimes our carnal mind gets in the way of accepting His love and understanding who we are. We are women who lack nothing. If you feel you are lacking, talk to Him about it before accepting that as your identity. He is true and just, and He will speak to you. Here are ten things that should define you.

1. Put God first.

2. Become a truth-teller. Say what needs to be said even though your voice may shake.

3. Walk in confidence, yet let your humility keep you grounded.

4. Walk in obedience to your God.

5. Honor your husband with faithfulness all the days of your life.

6. Rise for your family without hesitation.

7. Refuse to walk in trepidation.

8. Refuse to walk in intimidation.

9. Take excellent care of yourself.

10. Become a lifetime seeker of fulfilling your destiny.

Anything Is Possible

Think back with me about all the women in the bible, including Eve, who were mentioned in this book. Every one of them had a transitional moment where they were moving from their former reality to their new season with God. Imagine Eve just after God created her, her optimism and contemplation in God. She might have considered all the things that were possible for her life. Imagine Ruth, ready to embark on a New Journey with Naomi. She takes the first step on the brand-new road with curiosity and excitement in her eyes.

Imagine Mary, the mother of Jesus, hearing for the first time that God wants to partner with her and bring forth the promise of God. Think about that moment she felt in her heart and the thoughts she considered in her mind about thankfulness, discovery, and excitement. This is how God sees you right now. Just as He met with every woman in the Bible and brought them into a season of promise and provision, God wants to invite you into that childlike curiosity now. If you are in Christ, anything is possible. It doesn't matter where you came from. It doesn't matter what labels you had previously. It doesn't matter how many sins you committed in the past. Has He not taken all of that from you? It is no longer yours to hold on to.

With the World Before You, Who Will You Become?

Now, woman full of wonder, what do you want to do? With Free Will and choice, God openhandedly asks for your partnership. You choose to what extent you participate in this relationship. He has held back nothing for you. It is your choice, as it has always been your choice. Sometimes, we need gentle reminders that He is, in fact, the King who sits on the throne and that He has placed His Holy Spirit in us and upon us for such a time as this. Don't let the confusion abound any longer. Jesus gave you his Spirit; you are in charge of your life. We serve a relational God who has empowered us to do everything that is before us. We are limited no more.

The definition of love is probably different than what you've been told. Most of us grow up and think that love is a pretty dress on a beautiful day with flowers in hand. I must say, that's beautiful, but the true definition of love is Jesus. Every story in the Bible testifies to Christ. The pain, the suffering, the victories, the failures all testify to his love. Even the scars on his hands and feet and the lashes on his back all testify to his love. Do you not see yourself in him? Is it possible to define love without scars? I don't think so. God would love nothing more than to partner with you, shine His light upon you, and magnify you to the whole world. He will use every one of your scars for His glory. You are the definition of love.

Now is the time. Run the race with your whole heart and mind because there's a reward at the end. Don't let anyone stop you from the things you set your heart and mind to. Woman! Become all that you are destined to be. Unleash every gift calling, mandate, and promise He has given you. You are not to be hidden anymore! The world needs you to become the woman He made you to be! Woman, you are redeemed!

Milton Keynes UK
Ingram Content Group UK Ltd.
UKHW012151131223
434335UK00003B/32